COGNITIVE THERAPY IN GROUPS

COGNITIVE THERAPY IN GROUPS

Guidelines and Resources for Practice

Michael L. Free
*School of Applied Psychology, Griffith University,
Queensland, Australia*
and
Private Practice

JOHN WILEY & SONS, LTD

Chichester · New York · Weinheim · Brisbane · Singapore · Toronto

National 01243 779777
International (+44) 1243 779777
e-mail (for orders and customer service enquiries):
cs-books@wiley.co.uk
Visit our Home Page on http://www.wiley.co.uk
or http://www.wiley.com

Reprinted September 2000

Other Wiley Editorial Offices

John Wiley & Sons, Inc., 605 Third Avenue,
New York, NY 10158-0012, USA

WILEY-VCH Verlag GmbH, Pappelallee 3, D-69469 Weinheim, Germany

Jacaranda Wiley Ltd, 33 Park Road, Milton,
Queensland 4064, Australia

John Wiley & Sons (Asia) Pte Ltd, 2 Clementi Loop #02-01,
Jin Xing Distripark, Singapore 129809

John Wiley & Sons (Canada) Ltd, 22 Worcester Road,
Rexdale, Ontario M9W 1L1, Canada

Library of Congress Cataloging-in-Publication Data

Free, Michael L.
    Cognitive therapy in groups : guidelines and resources for practice / Michael L. Free.
        p.   cm.
    Includes bibliographical references and index.
    ISBN 0–471–98144–3 (pbk : alk. paper).
    1. Cognitive therapy. 2. Group psychotherapy. 3. Depression,
Mental—Treatment.   I. Title.
RC489.C63F725   1999
616.89´142—dc21   99–13725
                                                       CIP

British Library Cataloguing in Publication Data

A catalogue record for this book is available from the British Library

ISBN 0–471–98144–3

Typeset in 9/10¹/₂pt Palatino by Saxon Graphics Limited, Derby
Printed and bound in Great Britain by Biddles Ltd, Guildford and King's Lynn
This book is printed on acid-free paper responsibly manufactured from sustainable forestry, in
which at least two trees are planted for each one used for paper production.

To Paul Conrad

CONTENTS

LIST OF FIGURES

LIST OF TABLES

ABOUT THE AUTHOR

Michael Free is a lecturer in clinical psychology at Griffith University, Brisbane, Australia. He trained as a Clinical Psychologist at the University Of Canterbury in Christchurch, New Zealand, qualifying in 1980. He then worked for the Queensland Health Department in a variety of positions in adult psychiatry for 12 years before obtaining his present position in 1993. He obtained his PhD in 1997 for research on the relationship between biological and psychological processes during recovery from depression. He has published a number of research papers on depression. He continues to be active in research and maintains a private practice in Ipswich, a regional centre outside Brisbane.

FOREWORD

Cognitive Behavior Therapy (CBT) or Cognitive Therapy (CT) was introduced into the West in the late fifties. Since then CT has been applied to many psychological problems and psychiatric disorders ranging from anger management, anxiety and mood disorders to treatment of schizophrenia. Empirical evidence from the West firmly shows that CT is an efficacious therapy for many of these psychological problems and psychiatric disorders. For some, such as panic disorder with or without agoraphobia and major depressive disorders, CT is the treatment of choice. Not only is CT widely accepted and practiced in the west world, Oei, in his edited book in 1998, also showed that CT is gaining ground in Asia, in particular in countries like China, India, Pakistan, Thailand and Indonesia. Even though there are cultural, political and philosophical difficulties in practicing CT in Asia, the findings from these countries suggest a tentative yet strong trend that CT is also effective. It is now widely accepted by clinicians and researchers that CT is evidence based effective psychotherapy that has benefited many people suffering from mental health problems.

One of the reasons for the success of CT is the use of readily accessible treatment manuals in guiding the research and practice of cognitive behavior therapy. There are now many such manuals available from the literature and publishers. The earlier versions of the CT treatment manuals are based on individual therapy and have proven to be very popular and successful.

While CT treatment manuals based on individual therapy are commonly used, CT manuals in group treatment format are not readily available. Over the past twenty years my clinics and research laboratories have concentrated on extending individual CT to Group CT. We have applied Group CT to many mental health problems ranging from alcohol addiction to anxiety and mood disorders and have demonstrated the Group CT is just as efficacious as individual CT in the treatment of alcohol abuse, panic disorder with or without agoraphobia and major depressive disorder. It is with pleasure that I welcome this publication by Dr Free, describing CT in group format for major depressive disorder. A major strength of this book is its detailed procedures for guiding the use of CT in group treatment. The book is timely and will fill a gap in the literature. It is my hope that clinicians and researchers will welcome this book as much as I have pleasure in writing this foreword. My other hope is that this book will provide further impetus for continuing research in group CT and thus help make group CT as firmly established as individual CT.

Tian P. S. Oei
The University of Queensland and
Cognitive Behavior Therapy Unit,
Toowong Private Hospital
30 April 1999

PREFACE

In 1985 I started work at the Woodridge Community Psychiatry Clinic, which is run by the Queensland Health Department. This clinic was one of several new clinics established at the same time, extending the geographical coverage of community-based outpatient psychiatry in the Brisbane metropolitan area. I was the psychologist in the first team of mental health professionals appointed to the clinic. Woodridge was itself the centre of a rapidly growing new city south of Brisbane with many social problems and limited community resources.

I had always wanted to work in a community psychology clinic. It was four years since I had completed my professional clinical psychology qualification and I was considering enrolling in a PhD. Originally, my interest was in the anxiety area, but statistics for the psychiatric clinics run by the Queensland Health Department indicated that the numbers of people treated with anxiety disorders were too small to consider doing research on that particular population.

Depression was another matter. When I looked at the hospital admissions for the proposed catchment area of the new clinic, depression was the second most fequent diagnosis (after schizophrenia).

The second major outcome study showing the effectiveness of Cognitive Therapy (CT) (Murphy et al., 1984) had recently been published, further supporting Cognitive Therapy as an empirically validated treatment of depression. I decided that I would make depression my particular focus at the new clinic, and Cognitive Therapy would be the approach I would use.

I also decided to focus on depression for my PhD research. Working in a multidisciplinary team, I was interested in the relationship between modalities of treatment and their effect on different aspects of functioning. I decided to study the changes in biochemical processes that occur during cognitive therapy (Free, Oei, and Appleton, 1998) for my PhD research. For this project, it became necessary to develop a standardised cognitive therapy program.

Back at the clinic it did not take long before I had a reasonable number of depressed people referred to me for cognitive therapy. It seemed to me that it would more efficient if I started a group. I now had two good reasons for developing a group program for cognitive therapy.

I had previously been to a workshop led by an experienced local psychologist, Paul Conrad, who presented and trained the participants in a model of cognitive therapy that was a mixture of the approaches of Aaron Beck (Beck et al., 1979) and Rian McMullin (McMullin and Giles, 1981). I devised the group program from this model, with some format ideas from Lewinsohn et al.'s (1984) *Coping with Depression Course*.

The first version of the group program was just a series of points written on paper. The second was a series of handwritten full scripts for each session, which then became the first draft of the manual. Every time I have presented the group, and when I have received feedback from other therapists leading the group, I have refined the examples and language to make it easier to understand. I have also included people with emotional disorders other than depression in my groups right from the first one, and they have found the program as useful as the people suffering from depression. The version presented in this book is the result of many iterations, and nearly fourteen years of teaching the skills involved in cognitive therapy or cognitive restructuring to postgraduate trainee psychologists.

This book is meant to be a complete treatment manual, something that can be picked up and used with a minimum of preparation by a busy but well-trained clinician working within a professional setting. It provides such a person with all the guidance and textual resources necessary to run a psychoeducational cognitive therapy for clients with a variety of emotional disorders.

In an interesting twist, a psychologist from the Woodridge Clinic contacted me last month. He is currently reading a draft of this book with a view to running groups for depressed people at that clinic and in associated community agencies. He wanted something that would save him from the effort and expense of developing his own program. That is exactly what this book is for.

Michael Free
April 1999

Part 1:

Preliminary Considerations

Chapter 1

INTRODUCTION TO THE PROGRAM

SUMMARY OF CHAPTER 1

1. The nature of the program
2. The search for effective, efficient and ethical psychotherapy
3. Provision of therapy in groups
4. The psychoeducational approach to psychotherapy
5. Empirically validated treatments
6. Manual-based therapy
7. The relationship between therapist and patient in cognitive therapy

THE NATURE OF THE PROGRAM

The group cognitive therapy program contained in this book consists of full scripts for a twelve session group program of therapy aimed at identifying, challenging, and changing negative cognitions of participants who may be suffering from emotional disorders, including depression, anxiety disorders, and excessive anger. Each script includes instructions for exercises that assist the participants in accomplishing the tasks of therapy. The book also contains various resources to aid in conducting the program, together with extensive notes on how to manage the process of therapy within the group.

The program conforms to a number of trends evident in the provision of psychotherapy over the past twenty years:

- provision of therapy in groups
- use of manual-based therapy
- use of a psychoeducational approach to psychotherapy

THE SEARCH FOR EFFECTIVE, EFFICIENT AND ETHICAL PSYCHOTHERAPY

Psychological therapy for emotional disorders has been available for nearly a century. However, that therapy has not been available for all people, even in the countries in which it was developed. In Vienna at the turn of the century only the wealthy middle-class could afford to see Sigmund Freud and his colleagues. The same has been true for most of the twentieth century: many people who would have benefited from psychotherapy have not been able to get access to the service for a number of reasons. The main reasons have been as follows:

● people with lower incomes could not afford the fees charged by the therapists;
● there has been a shortage of adequately trained therapists in comparison to the number of people with appropriate conditions for treatment.

A major strategy to address these issues has been to make the delivery of psychotherapy more efficient and more effective, as well as to improve opportunities for people to obtain therapy, otherwise known as *equity of access* to therapy. In this discussion *efficacy* is taken to mean the quality of the outcome of the therapy, especially in terms of the symptoms and conditions the patients present with for therapy. *Efficiency* is taken to mean the value of the outcome in comparison to the resources required. Improvements in efficacy and efficiency are expected to lead to increased access to therapy because the therapy can be delivered at a reduced cost and more people can obtain therapy given equivalent resources. In addition, clinicians and researchers have accepted that it is ethical for therapy to be as effective and as efficient as possible. There has been an ethos within the profession of clinical psychology to evaluate therapy and thereby to improve its efficiency and effectiveness.

In addition to the ethical concerns, the economics of provision of health care services have become vitally important to governments and 'third party providers', such as insurance companies. In the physical medicine area there has been a move towards accepted units of treatment for particular conditions, and for health care providers to receive funding according to the mix of cases treated by their organisation. The same trend is evident in the mental health area, contributing to the imperative to improve the efficiency and effectiveness of psychological therapy.

Provision of treatment in groups

A major strategy to achieve efficiency has been to deliver therapy to people in groups. Perhaps the first person to seriously do this was the psychiatrist Maxwell Jones who found during World War 2 that he did not have enough therapy staff to treat the soldiers with 'war neurosis'. He found that he could treat these people quite effectively in groups.

The idea of treating people in groups has continued as the main paradigms of therapy have changed. Groups were developed for humanistic therapies, gestalt therapy, and transactional analysis. When behaviour therapy was developed in the early sixties there were many successful attempts to do systematic desensitisation in groups (e.g. Lazarus, 1961; Rachmann, 1966a, 1966b; Paul & Shannon, 1966). The same was true of cognitive therapy. Two landmarks in the development of Cognitive Therapy were the publication of the first major outcome study in 1977 (Rush, Beck, Kovacs & Hollon, 1977), and the publication of a treatment manual (Beck, Rush, Shaw, and Emery, 1979). Cognitive Behaviour Therapy has since become the dominant form of psychotherapy in most of the Western world, and is the framework used for most of the empirically validated treatments. It was not long after the publication of *Cognitive Therapy of Depression* (i.e. Beck *et al.*, 1979) that *Cognitive Therapy with Couples and Groups* (Freeman, 1983) was published.

The psychoeducational approach to psychotherapy

There are a number of formats for group therapy, including individualised group therapy, and group therapy in which interactions amongst all the members are regarded as important. Interactions can be organised by 'going around' the group to identify issues, by putting one person in the 'hot seat' who then becomes the focus of the group's communications, or they can be unstructured. The psychoeducational approach was one of the earliest formats used. In what may have been the first clinical application of group therapy Joseph Pratt, a physician in Boston in the early years of the century, brought tuberculosis patients together in groups to teach them about their illness and to encourage them to support each other (Rosenbaum & Berger, 1974, cited in Comer, 1992). Two psychoanalysts, Louis Wender and Paul Schilder, were responsible for initiating group therapy during the 1930s. At the beginning their techniques were largely didactic. Wender, for example used lectures and illustrative examples together with leading questions followed by discussion of the answers (de Maré, 1972).

The psychoeducational format is consistent with the ethos of behaviourism. One of the themes evident in the 1960s with the advent of behaviourism was the demystification of therapy, and the viewing of therapy as primarily an educational process. As behavioural techniques were applied to education, it came to be thought that this approach could also be used in therapy. It conformed closely with three of the philosophical values of behaviourism: it was procedurally specific, the active process did not require extensive inferences about unconscious processes, and it empowered the patients by making them to some degree responsible for the process of therapy.

The psychoeducational approach involves the application of a number of behavioural techniques to the teaching of specific behaviours that are seen as part of therapy. Its earliest recognised application in psychological therapy was probably in assertion training. In the first instance a task analysis is conducted of the processes involved in the particular therapy. The processes are broken into teachable steps. The therapist then teaches the steps by the provision of clear information as to the behaviours required in the step. The information as to the behaviours required can be by written instructions, demonstration, or provision of a model of the finished product. The patient then has the opportunity to perform the step and subsequently receives feedback. Performing the step can be by role-playing the behaviours with the therapist in the clinic, role-playing the behaviour in a simulated situation, or performing it in the natural environment. Feedback can include reinforcement as well as information.

A number of important behavioural principles are applied in psychoeducational programs:

- The information or prompting provided before or during the performance of the behaviour can be slowly faded or reduced.
- The behaviour can be shaped by positive reinforcement of successive approximations of the desired behaviours.
- Contingencies can be adjusted as the frequency of reinforcement is reduced.
- The contextual complexity of the performance situation can be gradually increased to approach similarity to the natural environment.

In addition to assertiveness training, the psychoeducational approach has been applied to a number of problems, including addiction problems, sexual deviation and dysfunction, anger management, and social phobia. A number of well-known and well-evaluated psychoeducational group programs have been developed for depression, including those by Sank and Shaffer (1984), and Lewinsohn, Antonuccio, Steinmetz, and Teri (1984).

Empirically validated treatments

Both the economic and the ethical stimuli for improvement of psychotherapy have had their most recent expression in the promulgation of 'empirically validated treatments'.

Both insurance companies and leading professional associations for psychologists and cognitive-behavioural therapists, advocate strongly the use of empirically validated treatments (American Psychological Association, 1993; King, 1997; Ollendick, 1995). 'Well-established' empirically validated treatments fulfil criteria including the following:

- a demonstration of efficacy in two controlled outcome studies conducted by independent investigators, and when compared to a placebo or an alternative treatment;
- use of a manual to guide treatment;
- clear specification of the client group for whom the therapy is intended.

A theme in psychology that supports the promulgation of empirically validated therapies has been the actuarial approach to the prediction of performance in outcome in a number of areas. The actuarial approach arose in part out of the need to predict success in educational settings. In many years of research it was found that the best prediction of academic success was achieved by regression equations based on the relationships between various predictor variables, including demographic factors and scores on aptitude tests, obtained in prior samples. Wilson (1997) extends this theme to the clinical arena: 'Neither the large body of evidence on prediction or decision making in general nor the sparse treatment outcome data in particular, provide support to show that clinician judgement is superior to an actuarial approach.' (p. 205)

The same logic, applied to clinical cases, implies that the best predictor of outcome in a therapy program is the fit of the individual to the set of characteristics of individuals who have been shown to benefit from that program in the past. In practice this means the DSM diagnosis (i.e. based on the current version of the *Diagnostic and Statistical Manual* of the American Psychiatric Association). Assignment to treatment on the basis of DSM diagnosis is in contrast to assigning the individual to treatment, or designing treatment on the basis of a functional analysis of their problems in accordance with psychological theory. There is considerable debate about this issue (for example see Hickling & Blanchard (1997), and Wilson (1997)), and this book is not the appropriate place to address the issue. The present program could be used both when a person has the actuarial characteristics which would predict that cognitive therapy is the treatment of choice, and also when cognitive therapy is appropriate in terms of the functional analysis of the patient's problems.

Manual-based therapy

Another implication for delivery of therapy has been the move to manual-based treatments. This development has had its source in a number of factors: the strong actuarial theme within psychology described above, the ethical stance of evaluating treatment, the need to train clinicians adequately and efficiently and more latterly the advocacy of empirically validated treatments.

Although it is possible to evaluate any therapy, it can be argued that it is much easier to evaluate a therapy when the procedures are clearly and specifically prescribed. It is then relatively easy to check that the example of the therapy being evaluated is indeed an example of the therapy it is purported to exemplify. It is also relatively easy to have the therapy conducted by multiple clinicians at multiple centres, thereby reducing the possibility of bias from the effect of individual clinicians or specific schools of the particular therapy.

It will be noted from the above discussion that 'use of a manual to guide treatment' is one of the criteria for an empirically validated treatment. This indicates the desirability of manual-based therapy, although, of course, having a manual does not in itself make a treatment better or empirically validated. Whether the treatment contained in *this* manual can be considered 'empirically validated' is difficult to say. In as much as it represents a form of cognitive therapy closely based on Beck's individual treatment it could be said that it is. In the next chapter an outline of Beck's theory is provided together with the specific aspects of the program derived from Beck's approach. The readers can decide for themselves how closely this treatment follows Beck's.

On the other hand, there are substantial differences in the format: the group-based presentation and the psychoeducational approach. The program has not been tested under the rigorous conditions required to be a 'well-established' empirically validated treatment in its own right, but two outcome studies have been conducted and are reported in Chapter 3. These studies do not fulfil the precise requirements even to be 'probably efficacious treatments' (King, 1997), but they use a meta-analytic criterion instead of a control group as the treatment comparison. Again the readers can decide for themselves how established this treatment program is.

THE NATURE OF THE THERAPEUTIC RELATIONSHIP

Rimm and Masters (1979) in the second edition of their text on behaviour therapy identified eight assumptions of behaviour therapy:

1. Behaviour therapy tends to concentrate on behaviour itself rather than some presumed underlying cause.
2. Behaviour therapy assumes that maladaptive behaviours are to a considerable degree, acquired through learning, the same way that any behaviour is learned.
3. Behaviour therapy assumes that psychological principles, especially learning principles, can be extremely effective in modifying maladaptive behaviour.
4. Behaviour therapy involves setting specific, clearly defined treatment goals.
5. Behaviour therapy rejects classical trait theory.
6. The behaviour therapist adapts his method of treatment to the client's problem.
7. Behaviour therapy concentrates on the here and now.
8. Behaviour therapists place great value on obtaining empirical support for their various techniques.

Fennell (1989) identifies the following characteristics of cognitive behaviour therapy (CBT). According to Fennell CBT is:

- based on a coherent cognitive model of emotional disorder, not a rag-bag of techniques with no underlying rationale;
- based on a sound therapeutic collaboration, with the patient specifically identified as an equal partner in a team approach to problem-solving;
- brief and time-limited, encouraging patients to discover self-help skills;
- structured and directive;
- problem-oriented and focused on factors maintaining difficulties rather than on their origins;
- reliant on a process of questioning and 'guided discovery' rather than on persuasion, lecturing, or debate;
- based on inductive methods, so that patients learn to view thoughts and beliefs whose validity is open to test;
- educational, presenting cognitive-behavioural techniques as skills to be acquired by practice and carried into the patient's environment through homework assignments. (p. 173)

The relationship between therapist and patient derives from these two sets of assumptions. It can be seen that these assumptions emphasise a paradox of a non-judgemental attitude to the acquisition and maintenance of symptoms or problem behaviours or emotions, and a placement of responsibility on the patient for unlearning the old behaviours and emotions and acquiring the new ones. The non-judgemental attitude and emphasis on responsiveness to the patient's needs and desires can be seen to be equivalent to unconditional positive regard, as advocated by Carl Rogers, and the explicitness of therapy can be extended to transparency in all aspects of the therapeutic process. There is also a demystification of both therapeutic content and process together with a clear emphasis on collaboration and respect between the therapist and the patient. The program presented in this manual is intended to be used in the context of the kind of relationship just described.

OVERVIEW OF THE PROGRAM

The program will be discussed in detail in the following chapters, but before proceeding with the discussion of theoretical foundations in the next chapter it may be useful to present an overview of the content.

The program starts off with an educational orientation to the main principles of cognitive therapy. In the first instance, a three-systems model of human beings is introduced which emphasises the interdependence of cognitive, behavioural, physiological and emotional processes. The participant is then introduced to the ABC sequence of Activating event, Belief or thought, and emotional Consequence. Participants are assisted to identify their surface beliefs over the course of the week between sessions, and to write them in the three-column format, one column for each component of the ABC. The second session includes a theoretical discussion of the role of cognitions in three of the main negative emotions: depression, anxiety, and anger. Once participants have generated a substantial number of ABCs, they are taught to identify negative schemas or core beliefs using the Vertical Arrow method. They then apply a number of approaches to achieving an overall understanding of the patterns and relationships amongst their negative beliefs, including putting the beliefs into categories, making a master list of all their beliefs, and making 'cognitive maps'. When the beliefs have been organised, the participants then apply a number of approaches to challenging their beliefs, including comparing them with objective reality, evaluating the utility of each belief, and constructing empirical tests of particular beliefs. The aim is that they will decide by these means that a large number of their beliefs are false. They are then taught various ways of changing their beliefs, including techniques that act by retroactive or reciprocal inhibition of the original belief, such as countering; a technique that uses an operant self-control approach (self-punishment–self-reward); and a technique that has a deconditioning component, voluntary cortical inhibition. The program finishes by discussing approaches to maintenance of the gains made in therapy.

Chapter 2

THEORETICAL FOUNDATIONS

SUMMARY OF CHAPTER 2

1. Background to the theoretical basis for the program
2. Beck's Cognitive Therapy of depression (CT)
3. Ellis' Rational Emotive Therapy (RET)
4. McMullin's Cognitive Restructuring Therapy (CRT)

THE THEORETICAL BASIS FOR THE PROGRAM

The process of developing this program is integrally related to my own development as a psychologist, and the major theoretical influences of my work. As with many psychologists of my generation, my first introduction to cognitive therapy was the Rational Emotive Therapy of Albert Ellis. The next major milestone was the excitement generated by the publication of the initial outcome study of Aaron Beck's Cognitive Therapy (Rush *et al.*, 1977), and the subsequent publication of *Cognitive Therapy of Depression* (Beck *et al.*, 1979). These events occurred during my training and had a major impact upon my development as a clinical psychologist.

In 1985 as a clinical psychologist employed by the Queensland State Health Department, I was chosen to be in the team set up to establish a new psychiatry clinic in a fast-growing population area of 180,000 characterised by public housing, major social problems, and paucity of services. A major mission of the clinic was to prevent hospital-isation of people with psychiatric disorders and to provide appropriate mental health treatment in the community. Perusal of the data available for the proposed catchment area of the clinic showed that approximately 25% of psychiatric ward admissions from the area were for depression. I therefore decided to develop an efficient and effective treatment program for depression.

About the same time a very experienced clinical psychologist within the Queensland Health Department, Paul Conrad, presented a series of workshops for psychologists employed by the Department. Conrad based his approach on Beck's theory as outlined in the 1979 text and also the work of Rian McMullin (McMullin & Giles, 1981). Beck's treatment was originally designed for depression, and McMullin's was for agoraphobia.

Thus, this program was developed primarily as a treatment of depression, and is based on Beck's theory as described in the 1979 text with some influence from Rational Emotive Therapy and McMullin's approach to emotional disorders. However, because the process of the therapy used in the program is very general, and is in part based on

McMullin's approach, it can be applied to emotional difficulties other than depression, in particular anxiety and excessive anger.

Since the 1979 text, Beck has further articulated his theory of the role of cognitive factors in the causation and maintenance of emotional disorders in numerous articles and book chapters. Key sources are Beck and Emery (1985) for anxiety; Beck, Freeman and Associates (1990) for personality disorders; and Beck (1987) for depression.

There are a number of reasons why it is important to articulate the particular cognitive model of emotional disorders that underlies the content and process of the Group Cognitive Therapy Program. In the first instance, no manual for treatment can cover all eventualities. There will be times when the therapist will need to devise a novel intervention to deal with a particular belief or behaviour demonstrated by a participant. Often a new intervention can only be devised from 'first principles', i.e. the theory on which the therapy is based. Second, as noted, there is no one external resource for the theory that underlies the program. Beck's model for depression is itself not a monolithic structure. There are a number of permutations that reflect the developments over the years, and include different aspects of the model. Beck (1987) makes explicit a number of these different aspects of the model.

It has also been noted that the program has been influenced by McMullin's Cognitive Restructuring Therapy and Ellis' RET. It is important to articulate the precise model that underlies the therapy so those therapists using the program can understand the content and structure of the program and thereby conduct the program more effectively.

Apart from the major sources of Beck's model listed above, there have been numerous attempts to present encapsulated versions of the therapy to orient potential therapists to the work. Often these are in major omnibus textbooks on clinical psychology treatment. Examples include chapters in David Barlow's *Clinical Handbook of Psychological Disorders* (Barlow, 1993); chapters in Hawton, Salkovskis, Kirk & Clark (1989), and a chapter in Mark William's *Psychological Treatment of Depression* (Williams, 1992). For different interpretations of the theories underlying this program, the reader is referred to these sources and to the original sources cited above.

The model of the role of cognitive factors in emotional disorders that underlies the Group Cognitive Therapy Program will be presented below, particularly as it applies to the process of intervention. As noted it is a synthesis of Beck's cognitive models of depression, anxiety, and excessive anger with the approaches of Ellis (Ellis, 1962; Ellis & Harper, 1975; Ellis & Greiger, 1977) and McMullin (McMullin and Giles, 1981, McMullin, 1986). Each will be presented in outline, followed by the main aspects of the program influenced by that approach. The final section in the chapter will articulate how the various theoretical models are integrated into the final package.

It should be noted that the content of this chapter is interpretation, not critique, of the various theories. This book is primarily intended to provide useful resources for therapists rather than to stimulate or effect academic debate on the many very salient theoretical issues that do exist in the area. Many of the propositions that are contained within the theories are controversial. There are often several different acceptable positions on any given issue. I have attempted to choose the interpretation that provides best fit with my reading of the literature, and with my clinical experience, which is most consistent with the overall model, and which is the most clinically useful in the context of a psychoeducational program.

A GENERAL MODEL OF DISORDERS

A useful way of looking at any group of disorders, and of understanding the clinical presentation of an individual patient suffering from a psychological or emotional disorder is in terms of predisposing factors, precipitating factors and maintaining factors.

Predisposing factors are events that occurred in the past or conditions that were present at the person's birth that did not directly cause the development of a disorder at the time, but which increased the probability of the eventual development of an emotional disorder. Predisposing conditions include genetic make-up, learning which occurs in childhood, and even physical effects that are the results of nutritional characteristics. Predisposing factors are therefore usually present some substantial amount of time prior to development of the disorder.

Precipitating factors are the events that are associated with the manifestation of the disorder. In the absence of predisposing factors they may be the complete cause of the disorder, or they may simply contribute to the development of the disorder, perhaps in conjunction with predisposing factors. Precipitating factors are usually events external to the person, such as losing a job, finishing a relationship, experiencing a natural disaster.

Precipitating factors can be sudden, such as a flood, or occur over a longer period, such as a drought. They *can* be internal, such as illness. Many models of psychopathology are *stress–diathesis* models. The diathesis is a weakness, a predisposing factor, and the stress is a noxious stimulus, the precipitating factor, that causes the diathesis to become manifest.

Perpetuating (or maintaining) factors are those factors that cause the disorder to continue to be manifest, once the precipitating event has occurred. Perpetuating factors may be external, such as the continuation of a drought or a bad relationship, or they may be internal, such as continuation of an illness. They may be a maladaptive behaviour pattern or way of interpreting social situations, or a lack of certain critical skills. Perpetuating factors may be continuations of the predisposing or precipitating factors, or may be new factors entirely. A perpetuating factor may be sufficient for the maintenance of the disorder by itself, or it may be contributory.

Interventions may address any number of the predisposing, precipitating, or perpetuating factors. A particular therapy usually has a 'primary premise' (Beckham, 1990) that it works because it changes one or more of these factors. The discussion below will identify the important aspects of the primary premise of the various theories and how these are incorporated into the program, or can be incorporated into the program by the group leader.

BECK'S COGNITIVE MODEL OF DEPRESSION

There are four major components of Beck's theory of depression. They are all cognitive, in that they relate to internal events that the person may be aware of, but which are not directly observable by other people. These events are not physical, as are some other events experienced internally, such as pain or hunger pangs.

The four components are *automatic thoughts, schemas, logical errors*, and the *cognitive triad*.

Automatic thoughts are a transient phenomenon. They include sentences and phrases that occur in the stream of consciousness, and images of various kinds. They only exist as long as the thought is in consciousness. A list of the characteristics of automatic thoughts is reproduced in Appendix 6 (OHTs 11 & 12), and is included in the material for Session 1 (Chapter 5).

Schemas on the other hand are permanent structures in the person's cognitive organisation which act as filters, templates or stereotypes to summarise the individual's experience of the world and enable him or her organise their behaviour. A list of common negative schemas is given in Figures 6.1 and 8.2, and OHTs 13 and 14, in Appendix 6.

Logical Errors are errors in the process of reasoning, such that a distorted conclusion or inference is drawn from the facts. Examples are making a general conclusion on the basis of insufficient data, or deciding that an event has a totally negative meaning, on the basis of a lack of positive meaning. A list of the different logical errors is reproduced in Appendix 6 (OHTs 15–18) as part of the material for therapy Session 2 (Chapter 6).

The Cognitive Triad is concerned with the *content* of thoughts. Both automatic thoughts and schemas have content, and logical errors act to bias this content to make it more extreme. In depression the content is mostly negative, and is about the self, the world, and the future. The result is extremely negative automatic thoughts and schemas concerning oneself, the world, and the future that are derived from logical errors in interpreting sensory data.

Predisposing factors for a disorder may be genetic, or may be learnt in the person's developmental years. Beck is not specific as to the role of genetic factors in depression. He does see that a biological state that comprises depression may have originally been adaptive in certain circumstances, and that therefore it may have been a genetic advantage in the evolutionary sense. Any inheritance pattern would therefore depend on the number of genes involved. Since the inheritance of a predisposition to depression is not simple, it is likely that a number of genes are involved and that therefore it is possible for individuals to have widely differing vulnerabilities for depression.

Beck is much clearer about developmental predisposing factors, stating that 'children exposed to a number of negative influences and judgements by significant figures would be prone to extract such negative attitudes and incorporate them into their cognitive organisation' (1987, pp. 24). The position taken in this program is that such negative attitudes are the result of learning either by operant or vicarious learning processes, or by interpretative attributions about the causes of events. The negative interpretations are facilitated by the tendency of the individual to make *logical errors* in the interpreting of data. These logical errors, or *cognitive distortions*, largely reflect the individual's tendency (a) to overgeneralise in a negative way from the facts, (b) to relate the conclusion to themselves in a negative way, and (c) to develop absolute, rather than relative, beliefs about the matter in question. I have grouped these into the categories presented in therapy Session 2. The interpretations are then incorporated into *schemas,* which are thought to be persistent structural cognitive entities, but which may be activated or deactivated. The content of these schemas can concern any class of experience a person may have, but of particular importance is the view of the self, the world and expectations about the future that the person develops. Beck calls these three aspects of the person's experience the *cognitive triad*, and states that an important aspect of depression is the negative content of both schemas and automatic thoughts in these three domains.

Thus a person, by virtue of the negative interpretation of developmental experiences, forms negative schemas about themself, the world, and the future. The experiences may have been objectively negative. The schemas may be conditional or absolute, as in 'if I fail at something important I am worthless'; or 'I am worthless'. Depression is then precipitated when an event occurs that is relevant to the schema and therefore activates it. For the example this could be a failure experience in an activity seen as important.

Once a person becomes depressed, the classic symptoms of depression emerge together with a number of aspects of the person's biological state that are currently not described as being symptoms or signs of depression. Beck believes that these act together to maintain the depression. Of these, the most important cognitive phenomena are the negative automatic thoughts. The negative processing and activation of negative schemas also continues.

It is important to note that Beck sees cognitive phenomena as only one aspect of depression. Other important aspects are the person's behaviour and physiological processes. Beck sees that cognitive aspects of depression are just one domain in which the clinician can intervene. It is just as valid to intervene in the physiological or behavioural domains. This idea is reproduced in the '3-systems model of the person' presented in therapy Session 1.

Core components

The following are what I believe to be the core components of Beck's theory.

- a tendency for cognitive processing to be negative;
- a tendency for logical errors to occur in cognitive processing;
- relatively persistent cognitive entities of negative beliefs and attitudes in the form of cognitive schemas;
- transient cognitive phenomena which are derived from the persistent cognitive entities in the form of 'automatic thoughts';
- content of these phenomena relevant to depression is negative with respect to the value of the future, the self, and the world.

Theories about the process of change in cognitive therapy

It follows from the above discussion that the primary premise of Beck's therapy is that cognitive therapy attempts to

- reduce belief in dysfunctional schemas, or to deactivate them;
- reduce the use of cognitive distortions/logical errors and increase the use of objective perception of events and correct logic;
- reduce frequency of negative automatic thoughts;
- reduce the amount of negative content in thoughts about the self, the world and the future.

There are, however, a number of views as to how this is achieved. Recently a number of writers have speculated about the nature of the change process in cognitive therapy, including Free and Oei (1989), Beckham (1990), Barber and DeRubeis (1989), and Brewin (1989).

Barber and DeRubeis (1989) summarise Hollon, Evans, and DeRubeis (1988) in describing three models of the changes which may be hypothesised to occur during the cognitive therapy of depression: the accommodation change model, the activation- deactivation model, and the compensatory skills model. In the accommodation change model it is supposed that CT modifies beliefs or schemas and/or the processes which underlie the creation, maintenance, and modification of beliefs. In the activation–deactivation model it is supposed that CT does not induce change in existing beliefs or processes, but instead leads to deactivation of negative schemas or processes and to the activation of more benign ones. In the compensatory skills model it is supposed that patients using cognitive therapy acquire a set of skills which they then use to curtail negative thinking both during the acute episode and while in remission following the episode.

Barber and DeRubeis further divide the accommodation change model up into two sorts of change: changes in content of schemas and change in cognitive process. They review evidence for change in schemas, and conclude that there is no evidence of specificity of effect of cognitive therapy in this area. With regard to the model of process change, Barber and DeRubeis consider that there is no logical basis for process change as such, but that most changes referred to in these areas refer to either change in valence of thoughts, or changes in the patients' skills in dealing with thoughts. They therefore argue that changes in processes are better construed as changes of these other kinds. Barber and DeRubeis also criticise the concept that changes in process during cognitive therapy relate to a change between automatic and controlled thinking and argue that this also reflects a change in compensatory skills, since the person does not become more controlled overall. Finally, Barber and DeRubeis (1989) are critical of other process-oriented models of change since they also can be considered to be either changes in content or acquisition of compensatory skills.

Barber and DeRubeis (1989) suggest that schema activation-deactivation is the process which occurs in the cognitive change which occurs in treatment by antidepressant medication. Barber and DeRubeis select remediation or development of compensatory skills as the means of recovery during CT, although they appear to include the modification of content as part of the process of developing cognitive skills.

A number of comments may be made about Barber and DeRubeis' (1989) position. First, they support change in the content of schemas as being the result of the application of compensatory skills over time, so the distinction is not clear (1989, p.452). Second, having attempted to rule out process changes as being a possible mechanism of change in cognitive therapy, Barber and DeRubeis propose that changes in cognitions occur in different processes in different therapies. If this is correct then it might be supposed that a person receiving one therapy might change processes when they commence receiving another therapy. It is therefore not possible to rule out change in cognitive processes as a possible mechanism of action in cognitive therapy. Third, the evidence for cognitive change is mostly predicated on changes measured by instruments such as the Dysfunctional Attitude Scale and the Attributional Style Questionnaire. The Dysfunctional Attitude Scale asks people to rate their agreement or disagreement with a set of statements that are thought to depict dysfunctional beliefs. The Attributional Style Questionnaire asks people to give ratings based on how they would think in a situation supplied in the questionnaire. There is also a third class of instruments represented by the Automatic Thoughts Questionnaire in which people are asked how frequently they thought the thought during the specified time period. The relationship between these instruments and the constructs they are purported to measure has not been established beyond question, nor is there clear evidence that instruments from one class measure the same thing as instruments in another class, nor even that instruments in the same class measure the same thing. See Segal and Swallow (1994) for a review of measurement of cognitive constructs.

Another writer in the same area who expresses concerns regarding the self-report nature of most evidence related to process of cognitive change during recovery from depression is Brewin (1989). He identifies three major problems in drawing any conclusions about the nature of the change process in cognitive therapy. In the first instance he claims the confounding of behavioural aspects of CBT with the cognitive such that the specific effects of each type of technique cannot be discriminated. Second, he argues that CBT has not yet developed a consistent theoretical framework, and third that issues regarding the validity of self-report have not been addressed by CBT theorists.

Brewin proposes that the object of CBT is to change 'rules' a person may have acquired, e.g. 'In order to be happy, I have to be successful in everything I do.' Brewin further argues 'it is generally supposed that rules can be changed by purely verbal means such as rational argument or altering what patients say to themselves' (1989, p.380). There is no strong evidence definitively supporting this as a process. Moreover 'there are unresolved questions over whether existing cognitive structures can be changed or whether new structures are created during the process of therapy' (1989, p.380).

Brewin goes on to propose a theoretical base for linking cognition, emotion and action, consisting of two cognitive systems, one for information transmission, and one for conscious experience, and submits that three types of cognitive change can be readily distinguished: rectification of misconceptions or omissions in a person's general data base of knowledge; modification of access to non-conscious situational memories that contain information about past experience; alteration of the conscious appraisal of coping options, teaching of new strategies; and encouragement of the use of the new strategies. He sees different types of cognitive therapy as being associated with the three different types of cognitive change:

> Many seek simply to provide information and to correct misconceptions about novel situations; ... other interventions, such as cognitive therapy for depression, have as their central feature the modification of access to nonconscious situational memories ... A final group of interventions are primarily aimed at enhancing motivation for coping behaviours, using such techniques as reattribution, problem solving training, and coaching inner speech. (1989, p.391)

In perhaps the most recent exposition of the principles of cognitive therapy, Beck, Freeman and Associates (1990) describe schemas as structures

> with a highly personalised idiosyncratic content that are activated during disorders such as depression, anxiety, panic attacks, and obsessions and become prepotent. When hypervalent, *these idiosyncratic schemas* displace and probably inhibit other schemas that may be more adaptive or more appropriate for a given situation. They consequently introduce a systematic bias into information processing. (p.32; emphasis mine)

Schemas are also thought to have structural qualities such as breadth, capacity for modification, and relative prominence in the cognitive organisation. They may also have varying degrees of activation from latent to hypervalent. It is thought that previously latent depressive schemas are operative during depression. When particular schemas are hypervalent, 'the threshold for activation of the constituent schemas is low: they are readily triggered by a remote or trivial stimulus. They are also "prepotent"; that is, they readily supersede more appropriate schemas or configurations in processing information' (1990, p.33). In this way, the negative schemas associated with depression result in a systematic negative bias in interpretation, recall, and prediction of experiences.

Depression can also be construed as an activation or cathexis of negative schemas. Beck and Freeman see cognitive therapy for depression as recathecting rational beliefs and that cognitive therapy 'aims explicitly to "re-energise" the reality-testing system.' (1990, p.37)

Integration of the above suggests that there are the following mechanisms of cognitive change associated with cognitive therapy of depression:

1. **Schema/belief/rule change**. Change in content of schemas or substitution of one schema for another, e.g. 'Father Christmas brings toys for children at Christmas' versus 'there is no such person as Father Christmas'.
2. **Change in cognitive processing**. This could be a change from using one of the logical errors identified by Beck *et al.* (1979) and Burns (1980) to more objective or scientific thinking, or the re-energising of the reality testing system mentioned by Beck and Freeman (1990). It might be argued by Barber and DeRubeis that change in cognitive processing fits with a compensatory skills model. It is part of their compensatory skills model that an outcome of developing compensatory skills is belief change. It is also possible that a change in the process of thinking occurs following the development of compensatory skills.
3. **Schema activation–deactivation** (Barber and DeRubeis) or change in the valence or prepotency of schema (Beck and Freeman), or the degree of energy associated with them. The former is a dichotomous model whereas the latter are models in which the prominence of the belief may vary on a continuum. If degree of belief is considered to be related to its level of activation, then this becomes similar to the content change model. Two other considerations are important. The more we view either activation–

deactivation or content change as being continua, the more they are similar to each other. Second, the more we are concerned with evidence that is accessible to us rather than hypothesising about the actual physical correlates of the phenomena, the less the distinction will matter.

4. **Development of compensatory skills** (Barber and DeRubeis), or development and application of new strategies such as reattribution, problem-solving training, and coaching inner speech (Brewin). This usually involves a degree of conscious intervention and is seen as similar to correcting one's backhand or switching from left-hand drive to right-hand drive. The new belief retroactively inhibits the old belief, resulting in one of the other sorts of change.
5. **Change in beliefs by provision of new information** or exercise in logic (rational disputation) (Brewin). This is the 'aha' phenomenon in which the belief change is instantaneous once the process is complete.
6. **Modification of access to non-conscious situational memories**. Brewin (1989) is not clear on what the result of this is. It could possibly be content change, deactivation, or process change.
7. **Reduction in frequency of negative automatic thoughts.** Automatic thoughts are supposed to maintain the negative emotion by being repeated frequently. Therefore reduction in frequency of repetition, either by conscious effort or as a result of other cognitive changes, should lead to reduction in negative emotion.

It can be seen that there are two clear clusters of these mechanisms of cognitive change. Schema/belief/rule change, changes in cognitive processes, and schema activation/deactivation are all descriptions of what might be happening inside the black box. In contrast provision of new information/use of logic, compensatory skills, reduction in frequency of negative automatic thoughts, and modification of access to non-conscious situational memories are all descriptions of the process the person might go through in order to achieve changes of the other three kinds. It might be useful to think of the processes involved in cognitive and other therapies of depression as being various combinations of these two groups of processes.

It is clear that these processes must be considered in investigating process changes associated with recovery from depression. It may well be that Barber and DeRubeis are correct that different processes occur in different therapies but with the same measurable result, but it is also possible that different processes or combinations of processes occur at different times in therapy. There is some evidence that the provision of therapy of any kind provides people with more hope. There is evidence that reduction of hopelessness is the *sine qua non* of the early stages of therapy for depression, and that some of the early results of cognitive therapy may be related to the educational materials provided at the beginning of therapy (Fennell and Teasdale, 1987). This finding may be evidence that provision of information results in changes in content of schemas whilst the application of compensatory skills taught in later stages of cognitive therapy may result in reactivation or acquisition of non-dysfunctional beliefs or reactivation or acquisition of more objective processes of information processing.

Thus it seems from a practical point of view that there are three main types of change which are supposed to occur during cognitive therapy. First some kind of modification of the more permanent cognitive structures, and second some kind of change in the process of thinking that is, initially at least, consciously and wilfully driven. The third change is from the automatic thinking of negative thoughts to the deliberate thinking of thoughts that are more consistent with objective reality. The last two of these are easy to understand because they are directly analogous to the process involved in attending to aspects of behaviour, discriminating between desirable and undesirable behaviour and changing the undesirable behaviour to more desirable. Examples are changing a golf swing or a swimming stroke to be more effective.

The first kind of change is the least well understood. In this therapy it is presumed that some schema change occurs directly as a result of provision of incompatible information. Other schema change is thought to occur as a result of the application of the cognitive skills, and by the deliberate substitution of counters for negative automatic thoughts.

Implications for the Group Cognitive Therapy program

The Group Cognitive Therapy program attempts to address all the cognitive aspects of Beck's therapy, but does not explicitly include behavioural components. The presentation of the three systems model in Session 1 recognises Beck's view that there are physiological and behavioural components of depression that are closely integrated with the cognitive aspects. It also provides a framework to incorporate cognitive therapy into a treatment plan that includes behavioural and biological interventions. The extensive educational component in the first two sessions aims at changing schemas through early intervention, and capitalises on the findings of Fennell and Teasdale (1987) that early positive responders to cognitive therapy are responding primarily to the educational component. Early stages are explicitly concerned with identification of automatic thoughts through the A-B-C model and the three-column technique. Schemas are identified using the vertical arrow technique. Logical errors are mentioned but participants are not specifically required to identify them. The various techniques for challenging beliefs are meant to develop more adaptive logical strategies. Finally, countering is supposed to provide a discipline to rehearse positive thoughts instead of repeating negative automatic thoughts

It therefore behoves the group leader to be aware of what aspects of the change process are thought to be involved with each component of therapy and to maximise the impact on these change processes. This includes such things as: making sure that the educational information is presented as clearly as possible, that the vertical arrows are identifying important and relevant schemas, that the person is learning the skills of more logical thinking, and that the person is consciously countering negative thoughts.

Anxiety disorders

It can be seen that a lot of the content of thought related to depression is concerned with loss or devaluation. Beck sees the causation and maintenance of anxiety as slightly different from that of depression. In talking about anxiety Beck distinguishes between fear and anxiety. He labels anticipation of damage *fear*, and the unpleasant emotional reaction *anxiety*. Beck believes that anxiety results from real or imaginary threats to ourselves, or to the safety, health, or psychological state of any person within our personal domain, or to an institution or principle which we value. Thus with anxiety the loss or devaluation is in the *future*.

According to Beck, two major cognitive events are associated with anxiety. They are both judgements that are made about a situation. *Primary appraisal* identifies the situation as a threat and assesses the probability, imminence, and degree of potential harm. *Secondary appraisal* is an estimate of the individual's resources for dealing with the harm. The balance between the two appraisals determines the perceived risk of harm and hence, the degree of anxiety.

The same sort of logical errors associated with the value of the loss in depression apply during the appraisal process and result in the individual making inaccurate appraisals, and therefore becoming needlessly anxious. In a process similar to depression, these logical errors lead the person to have inaccurate schemas about the danger associated with certain situations.

Implications for the program

Much of the material covered in the above section is introduced to the clients in the second session. Logical errors are also covered in this session. The vertical arrow procedure used in Sessions 3 and 4 is as appropriate for anxiety as for depression. Two of the stereotyped schemas identified in Session 2 are particularly relevant to anxiety: 'monster', and 'catastrophe'. Since anxiety is concerned with the future, the other stereotyped schemas of 'I stink', 'alone', 'kitten', and 'bomb' are relevant to anxiety when the person appraises a certain situation as likely to result in those particular losses, and that he or she does not have sufficient resources to cope. The techniques for challenging presented in Sessions 6 to 10 can be applied equally to anxiety, and the techniques for changing beliefs in Sessions 10 to 12 also can be applied easily and appropriately to anxiety disorders. In particular, voluntary cortical inhibition includes a number of the key elements of systematic desensitisation, and is therefore likely to be beneficial for persons suffering from anxiety disorders.

Anger

The meaning of an event is clearly important in both depression and anxiety. This is the central theme of the cognitive approach. The meaning of a sensory experience is separate from and different to the event itself. The meaning can be highly personal, and because people make the logical errors already described, the meaning can be false. In depression the meaning is about *loss*, and in anxiety it is about *danger*. In anger the meaning is about *transgression*, another person doing something that is *wrong* that has the potential to hurt the observer. According to Beck (1976) this can happen in three different kinds of situations: direct and intentional attack, direct and unintentional attack, and violation of laws, standards, or social mores. Beck also sees it as necessary that the threat is serious, and that the observer evaluates the thing that is being attacked as important. But the threat should not be so great that the observer concludes that they may come to harm, in which case the emotion felt is anxiety. Or if they perceive that harm has already occurred and it is a loss then the emotion felt is depression. Beck (1976) also describes the conditions that accentuate anger after an offence has occurred as follows:

1. The offence is perceived as intentional.
2. The offence is perceived as malicious.
3. The offence is perceived as unjustified, unfair and unreasonable.
4. The offender is seen as an undesirable person.
5. There is the possibility of blaming or disqualifying the offender (p. 73).

Of these, the third one is especially important, since often the cognition at the time of the anger is concerned with totally devaluing the offender.

Implications for the program

The Group Cognitive Therapy program is applicable to people with excessive anger. There are beliefs associated with each of the conditions described above. Those beliefs can be identified using the vertical arrow procedure. The common negative belief of 'you stink' introduced in Session 2 is similar to the third condition described above, and often occurs at the bottom of the vertical arrow. Logical analysis also helps people to become aware of the logical errors they make in setting the arbitrary standards, appraising the intention of the offender, appraising the maliciousness of the offence, appraising the value of the thing being attacked, and in judging the offender as totally bad. Many of the main techniques for changing beliefs, such as countering and voluntary cortical inhibition, are quite applicable to excessive anger.

ELLIS' RATIONAL EMOTIVE THERAPY

Rational Emotive Therapy (RET) was developed by Albert Ellis over the same time period as Beck's Cognitive Therapy. RET is largely a theory of the origin of emotions, in particular the maladaptive emotions. It is not a theory specifically of depression, nor other specific emotions, though as we have seen, many of the tenets of Beck's theory of depression can be applied to the other maladaptive emotions.

There are some strong similarities between the theories. Many of their central postulates are parallel, and the overall concept is very similar. The theories can be seen as complementary in many ways. In fact, in the *Handbook of Rational–Emotive Therapy* (Ellis & Greiger, 1977), the chapter on depression is contributed by Aaron Beck and Brian Shaw, who are both more usually associated with Beck's model of depression.

The central tenets of RET can be stated rather simply. Affect is thought to be the result of how a person construes an event rather than to be the result of the event alone. How the event is construed depends upon the personal beliefs about the event. Beliefs may be fairly specific to the event, or they may represent relatively long-standing patterns of thinking.

The beliefs are either rational or irrational. Rational Emotive Theory maintains that emotive disturbance is the result of the *irrational* beliefs. Irrational beliefs are those beliefs that do not follow, logically, from the facts associated with the event.

Ellis and Greiger (1977) identify four main types of irrational belief: 'awfulising', 'can't-stand-it-itis', 'musturbation', and 'damning' of oneself or others. Awfulising refers to exaggerating the negative consequences of the event to which the cognition refers. Can't-stand-it-itis refers to cognitions in which it is asserted that the person experiencing the cognition is, or will be, unable to stand the relevant event. Both of these types of irrational belief refer to concepts which Ellis believes are essentially undefined, that is the concepts of 'awful', and being 'unable to stand' something. He believes that persons possess unexamined and virtually superstitious referents for these concepts. The referents are unexamined because the person will not have thought through what 'awful' or being 'unable to stand' something means in terms of actual, physical outcomes. The referents are superstitious because the vague ideas and images that comprise them often refer to experiences that are worse than any which are physically possible.

The third category of irrational belief refers to a set of beliefs that may be interpolated between the event and events of the first two categories. Musturbation refers to one or a set of rules for the behaviour of oneself or others. The implication is that if oneself or another person does not behave according to a rule or rules, then it is awful, or one is unable to stand it. In addition, the rules may be impossible or virtually impossible to 'be' complied with, such as 'I/he/she must be perfect'. Ellis believes that the rules are essentially arbitrary standards that the person may have internalised from a number of sources.

The fourth kind of irrational belief refers to making negative judgements about the worth of yourself or others, sometimes as a result of applying the arbitrary standards of musturbation.

Ellis' theory is also applicable to anger. The rules that the offender is seen as flouting are 'shoulds' and are both absolute and often arbitrary.

The parallels between RET and Beck's theory are clear. Both refer to a distorted process of thinking which leads to beliefs that are inconsistent with objective reality. The domains of these beliefs are also very similar: they are concerned with value of self and others, and the badness or danger of particular events.

Influences on the program

The influence of Ellis' RET can be discerned in a number of areas. One of the most important is the 'A-B-C' mnemonic introduced in the first session. The influence of Ellis' thinking can also be seen in the set of common negative beliefs presented in Session 2: 'damning' of oneself and others and 'musturbation' are contained in the beliefs 'I stink', and 'you stink'; 'awfulising' is similar to the thinking in 'catastrophe'; and 'can't-stand-it-itis' is like 'namby-pamby'. One of the most important aspects of Ellis' theory is that it is the absoluteness of the belief that causes problems. The implication of this for the program is that it is not necessary to prove a troublesome belief completely wrong, just to reduce the absoluteness of the belief. This rule is important in the various forms of analysis introduced in Sessions 6–8, especially objective analysis and logical analysis.

McMULLIN'S COGNITIVE RESTRUCTURING THERAPY

Much of the theory underlying Cognitive Restructuring Therapy (McMullin & Giles, 1981; McMullin 1986) is derived from RET. There are, however, some important differences. McMullin and Giles (1981) contend that cognitions such as 'I must be perfect', and 'I am worthless' are neither inherently nor invariably painful. According to McMullin and Giles, the trauma elicited by irrational ideas is itself derived by means of direct or vicarious conditioning. This contention immediately provides a link with therapeutic approaches, such as systematic desensitisation, that are derived from classical conditioning models of emotion. It implies that deconditioning of conditioned emotional reactions may be a necessary adjunct to cognitive therapy. McMullin (1986) bases a number of his techniques on this, of which voluntary cortical inhibition (Session 11) is included in this program.

Crucial to the approach of McMullin and Giles (1981) and McMullin (1986) is the idea of *countering*, the replacing of the irrational beliefs with directly contradictory rational beliefs, which he calls *counters*. McMullin (1986) states:

> A single theory underlies all cognitive restructuring techniques that employ countering. This theory states that when a client argues against an irrational thought, and does so repeatedly, the irrational thought becomes progressively weaker. (p. 3; emphasis in original)

It can be seen that this theory is similar to the concept of reciprocal inhibition promulgated by Wolpe in the context of the deconditioning of classically conditioned neurotic anxiety (e.g. Wolpe, 1997), and similar to the fourth mechanism of cognitive change described above. It is based on the principle of retroactive inhibition established by the work of Bunch and Winston (1936) amongst others. Countering is presented explicitly in the program in Session 9.

CONCLUSION

This program is based on some of the dominant theoretical forces within psychology in the last forty years. It is hoped that users of this manual will incorporate further developments in theory into their use of this manual, until such time as empirical and theoretical developments render the manual obsolete. It will then be time to develop a new program based on the developed theory that is the result of the scientific process of hypothesising and empirical investigation. It is hoped that theory continues to develop, particularly with respect to the process of change in cognitive therapy. One particularly interesting area is the relationship between cognitive mediation and classically conditioned mediation of negative affect. Currently they are treated as separate processes with different manifestations, but this may not always be so. In a recent article Dadds, Bovbjerg, Redd, and Cutmore (1997) review the role of imagery in classical conditioning sequences, and tentatively conclude that mental images can substitute for the unconditioned stimulus and the conditioned stimulus in autonomic conditioning. In this program, images are seen as one type of cognitive phenomenon. If the trend invoked by Dadds *et al.* (1997) continues, it is possible that cognitive and classically conditioned phenomena will be seen as two components of the same process, allowing for a closer integration of aspects of treatment that are currently seen as separate.

Chapter 3

OUTCOME STUDY

SUMMARY OF CHAPTER 3

This chapter contains an outcome study of the Group Cognitive Therapy program. The study uses a meta-analytic criterion to evaluate effectiveness. Sixty-four depressed people completed the program in two intakes. It was found that the clinical effectiveness of the program in terms of change in scores on the Beck Depression Inventory was similar to that achieved in major outcome studies using individual cognitive therapy, though it should be noted that the level of depression at intake was slightly lower.

RATIONALE FOR THE STUDY

As noted in the previous chapter, the content of this Group Cognitive Therapy program was originally based on a combination of my training and experience in conducting cognitive therapy and a series of workshops presented by the late Paul Conrad as training for psychologists in the Queensland Health Department. The specific impetus to develop the program came from two sources. First, I was posted in 1985 to a new government-operated psychiatry clinic servicing a catchment area in which the primary reason for admission to psychiatric hospital was depression and related disorders. Secondly I was interested in researching the processes of change in cognitive therapy of depression and the relationship between biological and psychological factors in the maintenance of depression, and recovery from depression. (See Free & Oei, 1989; and Oei & Free, 1995 for reviews of these two areas.) In order to provide appropriate services for persons presenting to the psychiatry clinic and to study changes in psychological and biological processes during recovery from depression it was necessary to develop an effective and efficient treatment of depression. Part of the development process was to evaluate the treatment that had been developed.

In Chapter 1 the reasons for developing a psychoeducational group based treatment were reviewed, and in Chapter 2 the various theoretical foundations of the content and process were presented. The present chapter presents outcome data for a subset of depressed persons who have completed the program.

There are a number of studies that have considered the outcome of cognitive therapy, based on Beck's model, for persons with depression (Beck, Hollon, Young, Bedrosian & Budenz, 1985; Blackburn, Bishop, Glen, Whalley, & Christie, 1981; Elkin et al., 1989; Murphy, Simons, Wetzel, & Lustman, 1984; and Teasdale, Fennell, Hibbert, & Amies,

1984). The same results have been found in meta-analyses (Dobson 1989; Free & Oei, 1989; Miller & Berman, 1983; Oei and Free, 1995, and Robinson, Berman, & Neimeyer, 1990). As noted in Chapter 1 most of these were for individual therapy. There have been two studies reporting outcome for psychoeducational group treatments of depression which are less definitively rooted in the Beckian model (Brown & Lewinsohn, 1984; Shaffer, Shapiro, Sank, & Coghlan, 1981; Shapiro, Sank, Shaffer, & Donovan, 1982).

The accepted way of evaluating a therapeutic package is to compare the results for patients who are treated using the package with the results for patients who do not receive therapy using the package, that is a control group. Patients are randomly assigned to either the treatment or the control procedure, or in some cases to alternate active treatments. Participants in the control procedure might be a set of persons who do not receive treatment, or a set of persons who receive therapy after the comparisons have been made.

Free, Oei, and Sanders, (1991) have discussed ethical and logical reasons for not using a control group and standard criteria of statistical significance in evaluating a treatment program for depression. Free, Oei, and Sanders argue that it is unethical to put depressed people into a waiting list control and thereby deny them treatment for at least three months, especially when there are alternative approaches. It was therefore decided to use an alternative to the conventional control procedure in evaluating this program. Nietzel, Russell, Hemmings, and Gretter (1987), Jacobson and Revenstorf (1988), and Jacobson, Follette, and Revenstorf, (1984) have proposed a number of methods alternative to the traditional approach.

Nietzel and colleagues obtained scores for the Beck Depression Inventory (BDI) (Beck, Ward, Mendelson, Mock, & Erbaugh, 1961; Beck, et al., 1979) from a large number of studies containing comparison groups from the 'normal' population. Any post-treatment scores can be compared with the distribution of scores of persons from these samples using the formula devised by Nietzel et al. (1987). Pre-treatment scores can also be compared with these norms to determine the relative amount of clinical disturbance in the sample. Nietzel and colleagues argue that the method allows for a more relevant conception of the clinical meaning of the outcome scores.

Nietzel et al. (1987) obtained normative scores for two categories: persons from clinical groups but who were not depressed, the 'non-distressed' category, and persons from the general population. They located 28 studies from which normative data for the Beck Depression Inventory (BDI) could be obtained. In order to compare the results of clinical outcome studies with the normative distributions, a standardised effect size score is computed for each treatment group in each study using the formula $(M_T - M_{n1})/SD_{n1}$ and $(M_T - M_{n2})/SD_{n2}$. M_T is the mean post-treatment BDI, and M_{n1} and M_{n2} are the mean BDI norms for the two categories of studies used to obtain the norms, and SD_{n1} and SD_{n2} are the standard deviations of the BDI norms. Scores are transformed by these formulae such that they are re-scaled against the normative groups, with the scale being in standard deviation units for the particular normative group used. In contrast to other effect size measures, the results of this transformation are absolute values on the scale rather than reflecting the relationship between two contrasted groups. In this way pre- and post-test scores can be compared with groups of people with a clinical disorder but for whom depression has been ruled out, and with the general population. Furthermore, it is possible to compare the results of several studies when all have been transformed to the same scale. This approach provides a comparison standard that replaces the mean of the control group in conventional evaluation designs.

A criterion of effect to replace the conventional significance level is also required. Three approaches are appropriate. Jacobson, Follette, and Revenstorf, (1984) set a criterion of an effect size of less than two standard deviations from the mean of control groups as indicating clinically significant effect. Alternatively, the effect size obtained may be compared with effect size measures calculated for studies which did use a control group, or which used therapies of accepted efficacy.

Jacobson and Revenstorf (1988) have suggested a further method of evaluating the clinical effect of a program. Jacobson and Revenstorf suggest calculating a cut-off point at which a subject is equally likely to be a member of either functional or dysfunctional distributions. The formula for calculating the cut-off point, C, is

$$C = \frac{s_0 M_1 + s_1 M_0}{s_0 + s_1}$$

In which s_0 is the standard deviation of the normative population, s_1 is the standard deviation of the dysfunctional population, M_0 is the mean of the normative sample, and M_1 is the mean of the dysfunctional population. This chapter reports on the use of these techniques to evaluate the Group Cognitive Therapy program presented in this book.

METHOD

Participants

The patients used in this study were 35 from a 1987 and 19 from a 1992–93 intake. They were a mixture of people who had responded to media releases asking for participants in a research study of the relationship between biological and psychological processes in people with depression, and people who presented to outpatient clinics for treatment of depression and agreed to participate in the research study.

1987 Intake

Patients' ages were between 18 and 75. There were 10 men and 25 women, 23 of whom were diagnosed as suffering from definite major depression during the current episode, 6 as suffering from probable major depression and 6 were diagnosed as suffering from minor depression according to the Research Diagnostic Criteria of Spitzer, Endicott, & Robins (1985). Pre-treatment scores on the Beck Depression Inventory had a mean of 21.49 and a standard deviation of 7.736.

1992–93 Intake

Patients' ages were between 23 and 63. There were 13 men and 6 women. All were diagnosed as suffering from major depression according to DSMIII-R. Pre-treatment scores on the Beck Depression Inventory had a mean of 22.79 and a standard deviation of 5.86.

Measurement

The instrument used was the Beck Depression Inventory (Beck et al., 1979). The BDI was administered before the diagnostic interview, the week before commencement of the course, at 4 weeks, and 8 weeks of therapy, at termination of therapy, and at 1 month, 3 months, 6 months, and 12 months after completion of therapy (1987 intake), and at 1,3,5,7,9, and 12 weeks of therapy (1992–93 intake)

Procedure

The participants were depressed community volunteers, and psychiatric outpatient clients. They completed an intake screening, a diagnostic interview and then participated in the program described in this book.

RESULTS

Differences within the 1987 sample

MANOVA showed *no differences at pre-test* in level of depression as measured by the Beck Depression Inventory either between sites (university clinic sample vs psychiatric clinic sample), or between those who were receiving medication and those who were not. Repeated measures MANOVA showed no significant *differences in change in depression during the program* either between sites or between medicated and unmedicated patients (Free *et al.*, 1991).

Changes in depression

Changes in mean score for the Beck Depression Inventory are shown in Figures 3.1 and 3.2. The horizontal lines on the figures indicate reference points from the normative groups for these scales.

It can be seen from Figures 3.1 and 3.2 that depression has decreased markedly over the course of therapy, as measured by the Beck Depression Inventory. At the post-test the mean score for the 1987 intake was below the cut-off between depression and normal mood, as represented by the horizontal lines on Figures 3.1 and 3.2. People in the 1992–93 intake did not recover quite as well, with mean post-test scores on the BDI just above the cut-off point.

Figures 3.3 and 3.4 show the Beck Depression Inventory scores when compared with the norms obtained by Nietzel *et al.* (1987) for both non-distressed and general population control groups. It can be seen first of all that the sample was suffering from clinically significant depression, since pre-pretest and pretest scores are more than three standard deviations from the mean of the non-distressed groups, and more than two standard deviations from the mean of the general population groups. Post-test scores are within one standard deviation when compared with general population norms, and

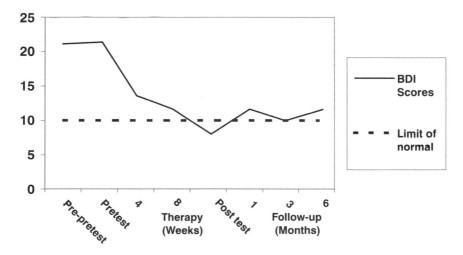

Figure 3.1. Changes in Beck Depression Inventory scores during therapy: 1987 intake

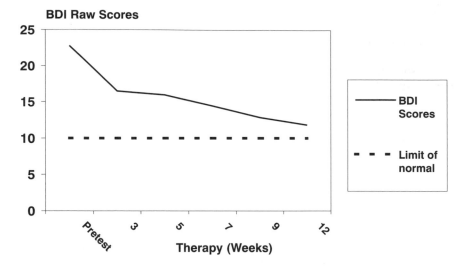

Figure 3.2. Changes in Beck Depression Inventory scores during therapy: 1992–93 intake

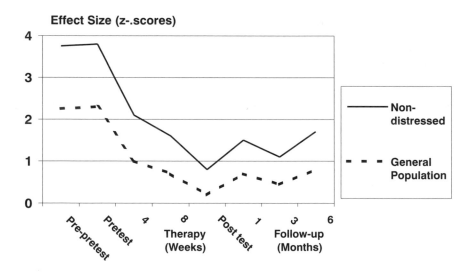

Figure 3.3. Effect size scores for the Group Cognitive Therapy program: 1987 intake

two standard deviations when compared with non-distressed norms which suggests that the Group Cognitive Therapy program is associated with significant change in level of depression.

Jacobson *et al.* (1984) set a criterion of an effect size at post-test of less than two standard deviations from the mean of control groups as indicating clinically significant effect. The post-test results for the program fall within the Jacobson and Revenstorf criterion for both the non-distressed norms and the general population norms. In fact it can be seen from Figure 3.3 that for the 1987 data the post-test effect size is less than one

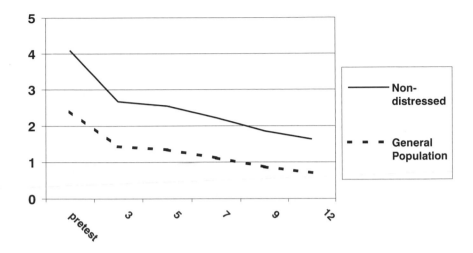

Figure 3.4. Effect size scores for the Group Cognitive Therapy Program: 1992–93 intake

standard deviation from the mean for both sets of norms. A cut-off point for determining clinical effect may also be calculated and applied according to the method of Jacobson and Revenstorf (1988). Using the mean pretest score (21.9) as M_1 and standard deviation as s_1, and Nietzel and colleague's norms for M_0 and s_0, for the 1987 data a cut-off point of 9.72 is obtained in comparison to non-distressed persons. A cut-off point of 12.79 is obtained in comparison with general population norms. For the 1992–93 data these cut-offs are 12.3 and 15.37. Using these cut-offs 23 persons, or 68% of the 1987 intake, recovered from depression to a degree that would be described as clinically significant in comparison to the non-distressed norms. 25 persons, or 73% recovered from depression to a degree that would be described as clinically significant in comparison to the general population norms of Nietzel *et al.* (1987). (There was no post-test score for one subject.) For the 1992–93 intake 9, or 47%, were recovered in comparison with non-distressed norms, and 13, or 74%, were recovered in comparison to general population norms.

DISCUSSION

It can be seen that the inclusion of persons suffering from RDC minor depression, the lack of a low end cut-off on the Beck scale, and the low mean Beck scores relative to major studies of cognitive therapy for depression mean that the level of symptomatology was more mild than that in such studies as Murphy *et al.* (1984), Teasdale *et al.* (1984), and Blackburn *et al.* (1981). However, it should be noted that there were many scores in the severe ranges on these measures amongst the persons treated in this study, and that a large proportion of the patients were persons who had presented to a specialist psychiatric service for treatment. The lack of exclusion for mild depression in the 1987 sample may mean that this sample is more representative of actual service users than studies which have excluded patients on the basis of low Beck or Hamilton scores. The ratio of males to females in the 1987 sample is typical of studies of depression which have included both but the balance is reversed in the 1992–93 sample making it untypical. The number of dropouts reported is very large, although most dropouts occurred before the first therapy session. The dropout rate from the first session on is comparable with reports of Hollon *et al.* (1988), and Simons *et al.* (1984). One can only speculate about the reasons for dropout but can note that there were a larger number of dropouts from the community psychiatry service than from the media release respondents. Patients of the community psychiatry service may have dropped out because the time of acute crisis was past, or because they did not wish to continue with the type of therapy offered. In any event, the possibility cannot be ruled out that the final sample may reflect a degree of self-selection of persons. Those who completed may have had a degree of intellectual commitment to a psycho-educational treatment program, and possibly to a treatment that helps them to recover from depression by changing their cognitions.

Premature termination of therapy may also have affected the results presented, in as much as results for persons terminating between eight and twelve sessions are treated as results for Session 12 in the analysis. Other authors have noted that many patients respond rapidly to cognitive therapy (Fennell & Teasdale, 1987). These people may be difficult to retain in therapy once they perceive themselves to be recovered. It may be that these people would have continued to improve before the end of the program if they had not dropped out.

Another important factor is the small number of persons on medication in this study. It was noted that there were no significant differences in response over time between persons receiving medication and those who were not. Moreover, it should be noted only a very small number had a major increase in medication at a time when it might influence these findings. The majority of patients on medication had been taking it for some time. It is believed that this reflects the usual situation in psychiatric practice. These comments only apply to the 1987 sample, since there were no people taking medication in the 1992–93 sample.

It is concluded that, with the exception of the gender ratio, the sample is typical of actual treatment users of outpatient psychiatry services, and probably reflects an intermediate group between primary care and inpatient treatment.

The results of this study show that a reduction in level of depression was associated with the Group Cognitive Therapy program. It is clear the effects of the Group Cognitive Therapy program were clinically significant according to the criteria of Jacobson and others (1984, 1988) for the majority of people. There appears to be some differences between the 1992–93 intake and the 1987 intake, in that a smaller effect on symptoms

Table 3.1. Comparison of effect sizes for various categories of therapy for depression with initial results for the Group Cognitive Therapy program

Study	Category	Pretest	Post-test	Difference
Free and Oei (1989)	Biological treatments	5.01	2.07	2.94
	Combined biological and psychological	5.16	1.03	4.13
	Psychological treatments	5.20	1.18	4.02
This study, 1987 intake (Free, Oei, & Sanders, 1991)	Group Cognitive Therapy program	3.80	0.83	2.97
1992–93 intake	Group Cognitive Therapy program	4.09	1.63	2.46

occurs for the 1992–93 group. There are a number of possible reasons for this: fewer were taking medication, and the therapists were less experienced and were using a treatment manual prepared by someone else, whereas the therapist for the 1987 intake was the author of the manual. It is appropriate to compare the effect sizes calculated for this therapy with average effect sizes obtained in the review by Free and Oei (1989). These effect sizes are compared in Table 3.1. (Only effect sizes calculated with reference to the non-distressed norms are shown since effect sizes for the general population norms will be the same in relation to each other but will simply be expressed on another scale). It can be seen that although the mean level of depression at pretest was milder than the average level of patients in the major studies, for the 1987 sample, the post-test level of depression was also somewhat lower than that achieved in the studies reviewed by Free and Oei (1989). Consistent with results on other indices, people in the 1992–93 group did not show as much symptom change as the 1987 group.

In the absence of a control group it is not legitimate to conclude that the improvement would not have occurred without the therapy. Nevertheless, the changes in depression associated with the program are within the range expected for psychological therapies for unipolar non-psychotic depression. Considering the gains in efficiency made by treating depressed or emotionally disturbed people in groups, it is believed that this is an acceptable outcome.

Part 2

The Therapy Manual

Chapter 4

PREPARATION FOR RUNNING A GROUP PROGRAM

SUMMARY OF CHAPTER FOUR

- Rationale behind the manual
- Acquiring appropriate resources
- Selecting participants
- Preparing prospective participants
- Conducting pretest assessment
- Understanding the Group Cognitive Therapy manual

RATIONALE BEHIND THE MANUAL

This manual is intended to be a resource for therapists wishing to do cognitive therapy with groups of participants suffering from emotional problems: depression, excessive anger, and anxiety disorders. The formal outcome research (Free, Oei, & Sanders, 1991, and presented in Chapter 3) has concentrated on clinical depression, but the program has been used clinically with people with anxiety and with small numbers of people with anger problems. It has also been used with people with sub-clinical levels of depression.

This manual provides therapists with a complete set of resources within a psycho-educational framework for a very cognitively oriented group-based treatment of depression and other emotional disorders. The psycho-educational approach was chosen since it is seen as more empowering for participants, and more consistent with the skills possessed by most therapists who would be intending using a program of this nature. The program is very cognitively oriented. I wanted to write a program that was a relatively pure application of cognitive principles; first because there was not one available, and second because I wanted to study various aspects of the process of therapy, and this was a more valid exercise with a narrow spectrum program. At the time of writing this program, excellent resources existed for other approaches. The *Coping with Depression Course* (Lewinsohn *et al.*, 1984) has an emphasis on increasing pleasant activities, the program developed by Lawrence Sank and Carolyn Shaffer (Sank & Shaffer, 1984) is an excellent omnibus program, and *Cognitive Therapy with Couples and Groups* (Freeman,

1983) is an excellent resource for doing cognitive therapy in groups in a more traditional format. (See Chapter 1 for a more extensive discussion of these issues.)

This program was therefore designed to fill a niche in which the major focus of the program was directed at identifying and changing negative cognitions. The program is aimed at people suffering from emotional disorders in which negative thinking has a major role in the maintenance of the disorder, either theoretically or according to the functional analysis of the individual's presenting problems.

ACQUIRING APPROPRIATE RESOURCES

The following are the recommended resources:

- Appropriately qualified, knowledgeable, skilled, and experienced therapists
- Suitable physical space
- Whiteboard/blackboard
- Overhead projector and screen
- Coffee/tea making facilities
- Ability to photocopy handouts

Therapists

Depending on the number of participants, one or more skilled therapists will be required. If participants are suffering from clinical level depression, i.e. DSM-IV major depression, it is advisable to have two therapists if there are more than four participants. One risk with even moderately depressed people is that a participant may report increased suicidal ideation. It is useful to have one therapist available to deal with this or other crises while the other continues with the group program. An ideal ratio is about one therapist to every three participants, but it is possible for experienced therapists to manage ratios of up to one therapist to eight or nine participants. The largest group I have run (with co-therapists) has been about 16 people, but I see no reason why groups could not be bigger provided the ratio of therapists to participants remains high. I have tended to work with up to four co-therapists, though these have frequently been clinical psychology trainees, and so have not been able to provide quite as much input as experienced therapists.

The lead therapist should be an experienced clinical practitioner with excellent clinical skills, including presentation skills, group management skills, and psycho-educational skills. The clinical skills include ability to monitor mental status and deal appropriately with increase in symptoms. The lead therapist should be an engaging and charismatic presenter with the ability to communicate effectively and impart a belief in the treatment but at the same time be non-defensive, authentic and transparent. The lead presenter, or anyone doing the presenting of lecture material, should be very familiar both with the program and with the theory on which it is based. He or she should be able to think on their feet sufficiently well to answer questions from participants.

Group management skills are also important. If the lead therapist is not able to manage the group then some participants will tend to dominate the group interactions and the group will spend excessive time dealing with their issues to the detriment of the concerns of others.

Some of the most important work in the program occurs in the exercises. All therapists need to be skilled at using the principles of antecedent control and shaping of behaviour by reinforcement of approximations to assist participants in acquiring the skills necessary to complete the therapeutic tasks.

Suitable physical space

The first requirement is a large enough group room to accommodate the number of participants. It can be set up in a number of different ways: In a circle, or horseshoe, or as a classroom with people sitting at separate tables or small groups of tables. A building with separate small rooms can be used, or in temperate climates, use can be made of suitable outdoor space. Since a fair amount of writing is involved, tables and chairs or lecture-type chairs with attached writing surfaces are probably better then armchairs. There must be enough space for the therapists to circulate around the group and not distract other participants when they are talking to one participant, and to allow a modicum of privacy for the participants. The space should not be so big that therapists have to spend a lot of time walking between participants.

Whiteboard/blackboard, overhead projector, screen, and ability to photocopy handouts

These are fairly standard resources these days, but you should check that your venue has them.

Coffee/tea making facilities

Each session lasts for two hours, and has been designed with a break in the middle. Even though the program was not designed to develop group cohesion as a therapeutic process, some degree of affiliation with the other participants is seen as desirable. This is assisted by having tea and coffee facilities to allow people to chat with each other during the break between the two sets of content. Even better is a separate area, in which people can have their tea or coffee and not disturb any participants who are still working. A break enables people to direct more attention to the second half of the session than if it followed straight on from the first.

SELECTING PARTICIPANTS

I have used the program in a community psychiatry clinic operated by a state health department, and in a university clinic. In both places evaluation was conducted and was reported in the previous chapter. To be suitable for the outcome study and the associated research (e.g. Free, Oei, and Appleton, 1998) research participants had to fulfil certain research requirements; however, people were accepted into the program even when they did not strictly fulfil the diagnostic criteria, but were excluded from the research data analysis. Thus people have participated in the program who have been suffering from anxiety disorders, intermittent explosive disorder, excessive anger, major depression, dysthymic disorder and various adjustment disorders. People suffering from any of these disorders are potentially suitable participants for the program.

A set of exclusion criteria was devised for the outcome research and other research, and this has been revised on the basis of experience over ten years. The following criteria appear to be successful in excluding people unlikely to benefit from the program, or who are likely to require disproportionate amounts of therapist time in the group:

- evidence of bipolar disorder;
- the depression is secondary to another major psychiatric disorder (such as schizophrenia);
- the person is currently abusing drugs or alcohol;

- there is evidence of major physical illness;
- the person has an identifiable personality disorder;
- the person displays severe suicidal ideation;
- the person has a history of organically based cognitive dysfunction;
- the person demonstrates reading difficulties.

The first four exclusion criteria reflect conditions where aspects of the condition are likely to make treatment complicated, and unlikely that cognitive therapy would be the primary treatment. It is possible that cognitive therapy may be useful as an adjunct with these groups of people.

Cognitive therapy has been shown to be useful with persons diagnosed as having personality disorder (Beck, Freeman and Associates 1989; Linehan, 1993; Young, 1990). I have had people with personality disorders in my groups, but they have not done well. It is also possible that they would not have done well in individual therapy of the same duration. In any event I have not included people suffering from personality disorders whose behaviour is extreme, or who are likely to demand excessive therapist time. I have tended to work with such people on an individual basis, although sometimes the sequence and structure of the individual therapy is very like that which occurs in the group.

Completion of the group program requires a degree of literacy and academic functioning in English as well as the ability to understand abstract principles, and I have found that people with organically based deficits in intellectual functioning or reading difficulties find it difficult to complete the program. That is not to say that they cannot do cognitive therapy, just that the cognitive therapy has to be presented in a different format to the one used in this program.

Finally, I have had mixed success with people whose first language is other than English, even though they may be very fluent in English. Even in such cases, it appears difficult to impart the concepts associated with cognitive therapy. It may be that the problem is cultural, rather than language based.

I therefore recommend that the program is used as a group program with persons suffering from the psychiatric disorders mentioned, and that people covered by the exclusion criteria are excluded from the program. It is possible to go through the program in individual sessions with people who fulfil the exclusion criteria, and I have had some success with this.

Prospective participants for the groups I have run have included ordinary referrals to a community psychiatry service, (including referrals from primary care practitioners), and respondents to community announcements seeking people suffering from depression to participate in a research study. They have then completed a two-stage selection process. The first stage is a 10–20 minute screening interview usually done by phone. The second stage is obtaining a research standard diagnosis by means of a structured diagnostic interview, such as the Structured Interview for Affective Disorder (SADS) (Spitzer & Endicott, 1978) or the Structured Clinical Interview for the DSM (SCID) (Spitzer, Williams, Gibbon, & First, 1990a; First, Spritzer, Gibbon, & Williams, 1996). The screening test was used primarily to screen people for the exclusion criteria, and to check that the person was indeed suffering from emotional or behavioural problems likely to respond to cognitive therapy. It was often conducted by phone. A copy of the screening protocol is included as Appendix 1.

I have used the SADS and the SCID for DSM III-R (Spitzer & Williams, 1985) and a version of the SCID revised at Griffith University, in conjunction with the Research Diagnostic Criteria, the DSM-III-R, and the DSM-IV. These interviews require a degree of training, and take between one and two hours, but result in valid and reliable diagnoses of a high standard. The decision to include or exclude a prospective candidate can be made with a high degree of confidence on the basis of the information resulting from these interviews. I therefore recommend the use of a structured diagnostic interview to select suitable participants for this program.

PREPARING PROSPECTIVE PARTICIPANTS

There are a number of stages in the preparation of prospective participants:

1. precontact information;
2. information given during the phone screening, or at the time of contact;
3. information given during the selection process;
4. information given after the selection process;
5. a special information session may be held prior to the commencement of the group;
6. information given in the first half of the first session.

Precontact information

The precontact information will include information given to the prospective participant by the referring agent, information the prospective participant has obtained from miscellaneous sources, and information disseminated as part of the advertising or media release. Prospective participants may have some general understanding of the nature of cognitive therapy and what problems it is suitable for. They may even have completed an assessment process in which cognitive therapy has been indicated as a potential treatment, either on the basis of diagnosis, or on the basis of a functional analysis. Appendix 3 contains an example of general information that can be provided to primary care agencies about cognitive therapy.

Information given during the phone screening, or at the time of contact

The information given during phone screening or at time of contact will depend on the purpose of the group. If the group is for research, then the information will include the research requirements as well as details of the group program. Appendix 4 contains an example of an information sheet that can be given to prospective participants about the format of the group program and general requirements.

Information given during the selection process

A certain amount of information will be given during the selection process. Some of it will be informal, either given spontaneously to the prospective participant or given in response to questions. The selection process also implies a certain amount of information sharing in terms of whether the prospective participant is likely to be suitable for the program and why or why not.

Special information session prior to the commencement of the group

If the group program is being tailored for special needs, or for research, it may be appropriate to hold a special information session. Such a session can present the research requirements in detail, allow for the asking of questions, ensure participants know how to complete all research requirements, and all monitoring procedures.

Information given in the first half of the first session

The final opportunity for the provision of information is the first half of the first session. This provides an outline of the structure of the program as well as some rules for individual conduct.

All of this preparation allows prospective participants to have as complete knowledge as possible about the nature and requirements of the program. The preparation allows prospective participants to make an informed decision about whether they want to participate, prepares them to some degree to accept the rationale of the program, and finally prepares them to function optimally within the structure of the program. It follows from this that all information is given as fully and transparently as possible.

CONDUCTING PRETEST ASSESSMENT

Schedule

In addition to the diagnostic screening and diagnostic interview, which form part of the pretest data, it is good professional practice to conduct pretest measures and to monitor progress throughout the program and follow-up period. A minimum process monitoring schedule is pretest, post-test and follow-up, but I prefer the following:

- pre-pretest (done at first contact);
- pretest (done prior to the first session);
- before the fifth session;
- before the ninth session;
- post-test (one week after the last session) (it is also a good idea to do one before the twelfth session since people can become less compliant with monitoring after the active therapy is ceased);
- one month follow-up;
- three month follow-up;
- six month follow-up;
- twelve month follow-up.

A vast number of potential measures exist. In the first instance there needs to be measures of the primary presenting problems: depression, anxiety, and anger. For depression and anxiety the Beck scales are suitable. The Beck Depression Inventory has the advantage that outcome can be compared against outcome studies by constructing an effect size score as is demonstrated in the previous chapter. With the move to the revised Beck Depression Inventory this will not be possible until a suitable base of normative data has been established.

Another suitable scale with excellent psychometric properties is the Mood and Anxiety Symptoms Questionnaire (MASQ) (Watson et al., 1995), which provides measures of two manifestations of depression, and two of anxiety, together with a measure of general distress.

Secondly, it is useful to measure the constructs that the therapy seeks to affect. Measurement of cognitions is fraught with difficulty and many suitable scales exist. I tend to use the Automatic Thoughts Questionnaire (Hollon & Kendall, 1980) and the Dysfunctional Attitude Scale (Weissman, 1978) though these scales are biased towards depressive cognitions rather than including thoughts that relate to anger or anxiety.

UNDERSTANDING THE GROUP COGNITIVE THERAPY MANUAL

The following eleven chapters contain the session by session instructions for the Group

Cognitive Therapy program. There is one chapter per session except for Chapter 15 that has the instructions for Sessions 11 and 12. The following broad principles were used in constructing the program.

- The approach would be psychoeducational rather than process oriented.
- Participants would complete a structured educational experience in which they systematically learned skills and applied them to a meaningful subset of their own problems.
- There would be a mix between didactic content and exercises.
- Participants would learn to work on their own problems.
- Difficult skills would be spread over several sessions.
- An important part of the exercise is giving the participants comments about their performance in the exercises completed at home and in class.

Structure of the manual

The manual section of this book contains two different kinds of text: session content, and guiding text.

Session content

The session content falls under the following headings:

- review of homework from previous session;
- lecture A;
- exercise;
- lecture B;
- exercise;
- homework for next week.

The rationale for the structure of the sessions is that the information necessary for accomplishing the therapeutic tasks is presented in the lectures, including examples and demonstrations. The participants then use the exercise to acquire and practise the skills involved in the therapeutic task under the coaching and guidance of the therapist(s). The therapeutic task is then continued and completed at home between sessions (or occasionally in the clinic), and since most of it is written, it is brought back to the clinic and reviewed by the therapist(s) at the subsequent session.

The *review of homework* section provides a summary of the homework from the previous session to assist the therapist in reviewing it. The section also provides specific guidelines as to what to look for in particular homework tasks. The two lecture sections provide fully scripted mini-lectures on the content for the session. The lectures are provided verbatim in informal language, though it is expected that individual therapists will adapt them to their own idiom. The lectures also include suggestions as to what the therapist *does* at various points in the script, such as showing overhead transparencies, inviting examples or comment from participants, or providing demonstrations of the particular task being discussed.

The exercise section provides instructions for carrying out the exercises. The main tasks of therapy are contained in the exercises. The presenter orients the participants to the exercise and then the therapist(s) circulate around the group coaching and guiding the group members.

Guiding text

There are five different kinds of guiding text:

1. goals of the session;
2. session summary;
3. session instructions;
4. background material;
5. problems encountered in conducting the session.

The goals of the session are presented at the beginning of each chapter, before the summary of session content. The goals are presented so the therapists are oriented to the key objectives of the session so that therapist efforts are primarily focused on achieving these goals. The session summary provides an overview of the session to orient the therapists to the session content. Both the goals of the session and the session summary are provided in normal text.

The session instructions are suggestions as to what the therapist does in the session: e.g. when to show overhead transparencies (OHTs), when to seek input from the group. These comments are in italics and indented to the centre to distinguish them from the main content of the session. Other more general background material is in shaded boxes. The material in boxes provides more conceptual guidelines, references to background material, and acknowledgment of sources.

Finally, the section on problems encountered in the session describes common problems that I have experienced in conducting the groups and some suggestions for dealing with them.

THE ROLE OF THE THERAPIST IN PSYCHOEDUCATIONAL GROUP THERAPY

One or more therapists may be involved conducting the group program contained in this book. For a small number of participants, one therapist will be sufficient. There are two major roles for therapists in conducting this program. The first is as presenter. The presenter is the person who presents the content to the participants, and who conducts the exercises. It does not have to be the same person all the time, and if there are two therapists it may be more interesting for one to present Lecture A and one to present Lecture B. The exercises can be also be presented by different people.

The manner in which the information is presented is important, both in terms of clarity, and in terms of engaging and sustaining attention. Most health professionals have well-developed presentation skills. The presenter should use voice intonation, nonverbal behaviour, and audiovisual aids to make the presentation as interesting as possible.

The other role is of guiding or coaching the participants in reviewing homework and doing exercises. A number of principles are important in both these processes. In reviewing homework it is important to be positive. Search for and praise the aspects of the therapeutic task that the participant has completed appropriately and correctly, and give information about errors carefully. Many depressed people are very perfectionistic and see any criticism as implying they are worthless.

It is also important to follow psychological principles whilst coaching people to do the exercises. Once the presenter has presented the exercise, which may have involved an example or a demonstration, then participants are expected to work on their own material, much as happens in a classroom. The therapists circulate around the group, helping the participants to carry out the therapeutic tasks. In helping the participants, the therapists can use the principles of behavioural teaching. The first time through, the therapist may work through an entire task with the participant, for example one Vertical Arrow procedure, or one Logical Analysis. The therapist may then get the participant started on the next example of the task, and leave the participant to complete the next step of the task alone before coming back to the participant to note and reinforce any progress. Intermediate amounts of help can also be given at appropriate times.

OTHER RESOURCES INCLUDED IN THE BOOK

In addition to the session content and guiding text, this book contains sufficient resources to present the program. Included in the appendices are a screening protocol and an intake protocol, information sheets, masters for overhead transparencies, and masters of handouts and forms to give participants. See the List of Appendices for details of these additional resources. Purchase of the book entitles the purchaser to make copies of the material contained in the appendices for their own use in presenting the program. It should be noted that the overhead transparencies and handouts were designed to be used at A4 size. They have been reduced to fit the format of this book and should be enlarged back to A4 for optimum effect. It may also be useful to enlarge the lecture text to A4 size to allow for easy reading when presenting it.

Chapter 5

THERAPY SESSION ONE

SUMMARY OF SESSION ONE

- Review of pre-therapy tasks
- Lecture A: Welcome/pep talk, overview of session structure, ground rules
- Exercise: Getting to know people
- Lecture B: Thinking and feeling; the saint, the standards we set for ourselves and others; the suitcase analogy for cognitive therapy
- Exercise: Guided relaxation imagery
- Homework for next week

GOALS OF SESSION ONE

1. For participants to accept that physiological processes, cognitive processes, and behaviour interact in human beings, and that emotions are made up of cognitive, physiological and behavioural components.
2. For participants to accept that most, or all, emotional reactions include a cognitive component.
3. For participants to be able to catch the initial surface thoughts that come between an event which produces an emotional reaction (an 'activating event') and the emotion and write them down in three columns, one for the event, one for the thought, and one for the emotional reaction.

Hand out, collect, and review pre-session process measures.

REVIEW OF HOMEWORK FROM PRE-THERAPY SESSION(S)

- As people come in, check they have filled out and returned questionnaires, and filled in any agency demographic forms.

LECTURE A

Welcome pep-talk

Welcome to the first session of this Group Cognitive Therapy program. For many of you,

you have taken the most difficult step just to get here. In starting anything new, the first step is the most crucial. In starting a new exercise program, just getting to the pool or gym for the first time is a major achievement. It doesn't matter much what you do there the first time. What matters is that you have made that first step, that you have committed yourself to something new and to some extent established the pattern. You now have to keep going with the pattern and to continue to work hard to get the best from the program. It will be hard at first, but the end product will be a you who is more emotionally fit, and more able to achieve and enjoy life than ever before.

Introduction

This introduction is quite important. The most important points are the emphasis on responsibility, that the participant rather than the therapist has responsibility for their emotional functioning and the introduction of ground rules for behaviour in the group. Most people will probably not remember the ground rules. Talkative people will not be less talkative, having heard the rules once, and reticent people will not become less reticent. Having mentioned the rules at the beginning does mean that they can be repeated and used to mould the group's behaviour over subsequent sessions. For example the group leader can say 'I'd just like to remind you that one of our ground rules is ...' In addition, the theme of individual responsibility can be emphasised throughout the program.

Before we start the main content, I am going to talk a little about how we are going to present the program to you. The program consists of 12 sessions of about two hours each. These sessions will be held weekly in this room.

Revise the following according to local conditions:

You may come into the room as soon as you arrive, if you would rather do that than sit in the waiting area. You may make yourself a cold or hot drink with the facilities available.

This program is suitable for some people who have anxiety problems, who have anger management problems, or who are depressed. It is based on the idea that emotional disturbance is caused and kept going by the ways which people have learnt to think about the things which happen to them.

The group is concerned with:

- explaining the idea that our feelings are caused by our thoughts;
- teaching people to analyse their thoughts;
- teaching people to find out about their problem ways of thinking;
- teaching people to change those problem ways of thinking.

There are a number of other important things you need to know about the program.

The following section draws heavily on ideas presented in Lewinsohn et al., (1984).

The Group Cognitive Therapy program is not an encounter group, it is a psycho-educational group program, so is more like going to an evening class on cookery or wood-carving than the sort of rap-group or therapy group you see in Hollywood movies or which some of you may have experienced. The main activity is that you learn new skills with the assistance of the group leaders and then apply these skills to your own material in class time, at home by doing homework, and then in the rest of your lives.

Extensive discussion of your own emotional experiences with the whole group is not

encouraged nor expected. Rather, group time is best used to address technical questions on how to acquire the various skills. I may from time to time use examples from group members' work. Participants will always be asked for permission before an example from their lives is discussed.

Homework is essential. It is not possible to do all the work necessary in class time. The more homework you do, the more you are likely to benefit from the program, and since each step builds on the one before, if you do not complete the homework you will fall behind. If you are having difficulties it is important to talk to one of the group leaders as soon as possible.

The responsibility is yours! You, the participants, are responsible for learning the new skills, doing the homework, and applying the results in your own lives. The group leader is responsible for presenting the material in a professional and understandable manner and for providing all possible assistance to enable participants to learn the skills. It may be possible to provide individual sessions from time to time to people having difficulties with specific aspects of the program.

The structure of the session. Each session consists of the following:

1. Filling out the mood-monitoring questionnaires.
2. Review and discussion of the previous week's homework.
3. A lecture based on new work, called 'Lecture A'.
4. An exercise based on the new material, carried out in pairs, the large group, small groups, or individually.
5. A coffee break.
6. Another lecture, 'Lecture B'.
7. Another exercise.
8. Setting homework for the next week.

> *There may also be time for further discussion, and if necessary it may be appropriate to mention that participants are expected to help clean up after the coffee.*

Questionnaires. The mood monitoring questionnaires will be set out in the room at the beginning of each session. There will be either one or two of them. You may start filling them out as soon as you come into the room for the session. It helps if you can be about ten minutes early so you can settle yourself down, fill in these questionnaires, and be ready to start the session on time.

Every four weeks, I will give you a more extensive set of questionnaires to fill out at home and bring to the next session. I will also invite you to attend follow-up sessions at one month, three months, and six months after the course is finished. These sessions will help you to maintain your gains after the course is finished.

There are several reasons for the questionnaires:

1. to monitor your emotional functioning;
2. to see how much the course is affecting your emotions and your ways of thinking;
3. to see how effective the course is in general;
4. to get information for future exercises.

> A discussion of instruments to monitor therapeutic progress is contained in Chapter 4. I think it is important to have a quick, easy and sensitive instrument that can be repeated each week. For clinical purposes I now use the revised Beck Depression Inventory or the Mood and Anxiety Symptom Questionnaire (MASQ) (Watson & Clark, 1991) to monitor depression weekly, and the ATQ and DAS to monitor negative thinking every four weeks.

Ground rules

> The following section is also extensively based on Lewinsohn, Antonuccio, Stein-metz, & Teri (1984).

Most psychologists who do therapy in groups have found it necessary to set some ground rules at the beginning of a program. This helps the sessions to run smoothly so that the time is used to the best benefit of all. The ground rules for the Group Cognitive Therapy Program are designed to facilitate the learning process and allow everyone an equal chance to take part in class activities and discussions. I hope you will all agree to the following four ground rules.

Avoid negative talk. A group like this can easily flounder in its own negativity. Try to keep any conversation to the task you are working on rather than all the bad things, which may be going on in your lives.

Be supportive. It is important not to get irritated or angry with other people in the group. People understand different things in different ways. We would appreciate it if you would be as helpful to other participants as you can. Some of you may wish to get together outside of class time to work on the exercises. We support that so long as it does not take away from the group as a whole.

Provide equal time. So that everyone can benefit from the course, everyone should have an opportunity to share ideas, ask questions, and discuss difficulties that they encounter with the techniques. So try to allow everyone equal time. If you are the sort of person who is always talking, then it would help if you try to restrain yourself some-times to give others a go, and if you are a shy quiet person, this group is an excellent opportunity for you to try speaking up.

Confidentiality. It is important to respect the confidentiality of personal information that is provided in group sessions. You are expected not to discuss information relating to personal matters of other participants with *anyone*, not even your family at home. Of course you are welcome to discuss with anyone your own progress, the particular skills, or the approach as a whole.

So that finishes off the preliminary material. We'll now do a short exercise and then have a short break. But first, are there any questions or comments so far?

EXERCISE: GETTING TO KNOW EACH OTHER

We are going to be spending some fairly large blocks of time together in the next three months. Even though this is a psychoeducational group and is concerned with you learning new skills, rather than exploring each other in depth, there is still plenty of opportunity to interact with the other participants. This exercise will help you get started.

All I want you to do, right where you're sitting, is just to tell the other members of the group your first name, and three other fairly superficial pieces of information about yourself.

> *Model three fairly superficial items about yourself, e.g. 'My name is Michael, I am married with three children and I live in a hundred-year-old house.' Then go round the group encouraging them to say their three things. After that, go immediately to the coffee break. The exercise will have given them some material to start conversa-tions with each other.*

LECTURE B

Thinking and feeling

> Research has shown that one of the most powerful aspects of cognitive therapy is the educational section (Fennell & Teasdale, 1987). In this section the important things to emphasise, and ensure the participants understand, are the interactive nature of the three systems, and the idea that beliefs or thoughts come between sensation and emotion.

Show OHT 1 or draw diagram of three systems model as in Figure 5.1.

Most of you are here because you have difficulties with one or more of the negative emotions: depression, anxiety, anger, so it makes sense that we consider how your emotions work very carefully. This is a diagram of how your emotions work. You can think of a person as being made up of three parts, or systems. One part is what you *think*, another is what you *do*, or your behaviour, and the other is your *physiology*, which is the chemical processes that go on in your body.

Thinking includes such things as the stream of consciousness, or conversation, which goes on in your head; it includes images and memories, and it includes daydreams. Thinking also includes things called automatic thoughts, attitudes, rules of behaviour, and beliefs, all of which we will talk about later.

Behaviour includes all the things we do, and all the movements we make. It includes tensing a single muscle group, tensing yourself right up, being totally relaxed, and it includes complex actions like making a cup of tea, avoiding your boss, or hitting your partner.

Physiology includes such things as the amount of adrenalin in your blood, the lactic acid build up in your muscles, the amount of carbon dioxide in your blood.

Each of these systems can affect each other. If we run or do exercise we build up lactic

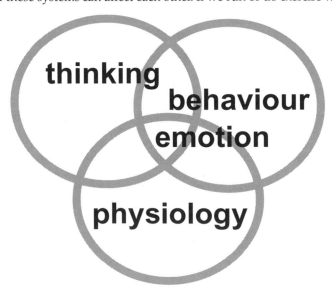

Figure 5.1. The Three Systems Model of human emotion

acid. If we hyperventilate we lower the carbon dioxide in our blood. If we change our physiology by taking a drug, Valium for instance, our muscles relax.

Modify picture as shown.

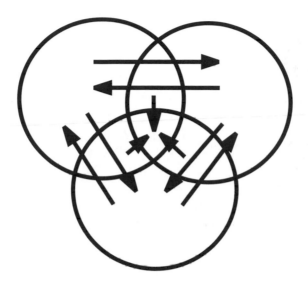

Figure 5.2. Each system affects the others

In the same way if we *think* about something frightening, whether it is a memory or imagined, we get similar physiological reactions to those we would have if the event actually happened. Changes in our physiology and our behaviour can affect what we think, too. If we take Valium we might think 'how relaxed I am', or if we do a lot of exercise we think 'I'm tired'.

So you can see that there are three main systems involved in emotional functioning, and in the middle of them all is *emotion*, or what we feel. Emotion, then, is really made up of what we do, what we think, and the physiological processes going on in our bodies.

So how does this relate to the world outside our bodies? We experience the world outside through the traditional five senses: sight, hearing, touch, smell, and taste, and we also experience our internal world and the way our body moves in the external world. The internal world is especially important to anxiety sufferers, as we shall see. But you can see from the diagram that sensation does not influence emotion directly, because emotion is in the middle. Cognitive therapists believe that there is always some *cognitive processing*, or *thinking*, or interpretation, which comes between an event and the emotion which we feel in response.

For example we get scared when someone is coming toward us with a knife, *if* we *think* the person is going to do us some harm. We *don't* get scared if we think the person is simply coming to carve the roast dinner.

Show OHT of referee whistling (OHT 3).

We experience different emotions when the referee blows his whistle, depending on whether we think the penalty is fair or not.

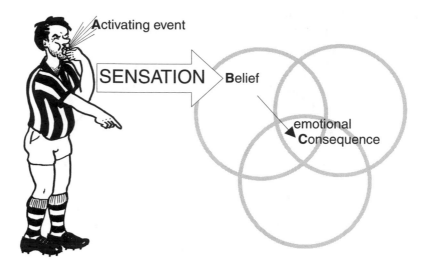

Figure 5.3 The A-B-C model of emotion. ('Referee' by V. Parslow-Stafford)

We call this the A-B-C model of emotion, and it is the most important thing for you to learn today. A is for *activating event*, B is for *belief*, or thought, and C is for emotional *consequence*, which just means the emotion you feel. Albert Ellis, whose thinking underlies much of what is being presented in this program, first described the model in this form.

There can be lots of different kinds of As, Bs, and Cs. An example of an A can be an event such as seeing a snake, the death of a loved one, or they can be summaries of events: 'My mother never shows me any affection'; 'Jill has been out the last five times I've called her'; or even thoughts can be activating events. Thinking about your mother might lead to other thoughts and then emotion, for instance. For the anxious person the events can be internal experiences such as noticing your heart beating rapidly, or feeling light-headed.

There can be different kinds of Bs, too. Bs can be beliefs or attitudes, such as 'a real man can provide for his family'; they can be visual images, like an image of your father standing over you; or kinaesthetic images, such as the feeling of being pushed under. They can be short, brief automatic thoughts such as 'I'll be no good at this'; or general statements or core beliefs, such as 'I'm no good'.

Finally, there can be lots of different kinds of Cs, or emotions. In this course we'll mostly be dealing with the negative emotions of depression, anxiety, and anger, or variants of these. Let's look at some examples of the A-B-C sequence now.

We probably all remember being frightened by shadows and things when we were children, especially at night when we were in bed. The moonlight can make different shadows at different times, and these can look to a child like a monster or a wolf, for example. Now of course it isn't really a monster or a wolf causing the fear, and it's not the shadow, because shadows can't harm you. What causes the fear is the way you thought about the shadow: 'that's a monster and it's going to eat me', for instance.

In looking at examples of the A-B-C sequence we are working towards the participants eventually being able to identify their own changes in emotions and the events and thoughts associated with them. You will note that the process is introduced by having participants identify possible thoughts and feelings for *other* people. I have found it much easier to develop the skill in this way using a third person approach, rather than initially considering their own beliefs, because it avoids the defensiveness which occurs when one uses the participants' own events and emotions. Moreover we are trying to introduce the idea that sometimes the thoughts which emotions are based on are false. People usually find it easier to generate alternative beliefs and recognise irrational thinking in other people. I therefore strongly recommend the 'third person' approach.

In the same way, if we hear a noise in the night, and we think it is going to cause us harm, then we get frightened. But if we think that the noise is the neighbour's cat, or a possum on the roof, then we don't get frightened.

Present OHT 4 or draw or as shown in Figure 5.4.

Activating Event	Belief or thought	emotional Consequence

Figure 5.4 The three-column format

Put examples (wolf-shadow, noise on roof, and others below) into the three column format. Use OHTs 4–8. Engage the class by asking 'what different thoughts might a person have in this situation, what would another person think when seeing the situation?' Generate different Bs and Cs for the same activating event as suggested, either for different people or for the same person.

Another example might be two people who overeat one night. Both wake up the next morning feeling very sick. One person might panic and go to the doctor thinking 'I've got food poisoning, I might die'. The other might think 'red wine and chocolate again, I should be more careful', and simply take it easy for the day. The way the two people thought about their sickness determined their feelings, and also what they did.

Or imagine two people getting ready for a party (OHT 5). One person is worrying about what he or she is going to say, and what people are going to think of him or her. How do you think that person is going to feel?

Encourage discussion. Continue to put into the three column format.

Another person getting ready for the same party is thinking of what an interesting time he or she is going to have and that he or she might meet someone nice there. How is this person going to feel?

All of these examples so far have been to do with anxiety. Anxiety usually comes from thoughts of danger, or harm, which may not be correct. The other major problem emotion is depression. Depression usually comes when we think we have lost something. Imagine two people who have just broken a vase. In one case the person didn't really like the vase, in the other it was something given by a favourite aunt. How do you think the first person is going to feel? The second person?

As before encourage discussion and demonstrate if necessary.

Let's look at some other examples:

Encourage discussion and demonstrate in A-B-C columns. Continue to use third person examples until the participants are able to generate alternative beliefs, and associated emotions for given situations, and are able to put correct information in the various columns.

1. A Boss yells. The employee thinks 'that swine has a nerve yelling at me. I don't have to stand for this.' What would the employee's 'C' be? *Or* ... Boss Yells. Employee thinks 'the boss is yelling at me again. I can't do anything right. How useless I am.' What would the employee's 'C' be in this case?
2. A person is giving a speech and a member of the audience gets up and leaves. What different Bs might the speaker have? What different Cs?
3. A person is walking in the street and an old acquaintance passes by. What different Bs could the passed-by person have? What would be his/her Cs?
4. A person wakes up in the morning, looks around and feels depressed. What thoughts might that person have had? What thoughts might another person have?

Can you think of other examples of when what a person feels is obviously caused by what he or she thinks, either with a friend, acquaintance, public figure?

Elicit more third person examples. It may then be possible to elicit some recent occasions on which participants have felt angry, depressed, or anxious, and write them down in the A-B-C sequence. It is better to use fairly innocuous and uncomplicated examples to begin with. Try to get a good range of types of As and Bs, and Cs. Then get people to write down several A-B-C situations on their own. There is a blank three column table on OHT 8 you can use for other A-B-Cs.

Now you can see that the way different people thought about the same activating event determined the emotional consequence they experienced, and for some of them that emotional consequence was unpleasant. What if we could change the beliefs of the people who suffered the negative emotions to the beliefs of the people who experienced positive or neutral emotions, it would be good for those people, wouldn't it? Well that's what this program is about. We'll talk about that in detail in a short while, but first we're going to consider why we experience some of those negative emotions.

The saint and the checklist

So far we have been talking about how we feel emotions in general, but in this course we are not concerned with all the positive emotions, but just the ones that get us into trouble, and make us feel bad. It's important to realise that we are not trying to say that any emotion is bad, or trying to teach you to become unfeeling robots, but rather to help you to deal with and control (to some extent), the emotions which lead to your life difficulties. For the rest of this session, and for most of the next session, I will be talking about how we come to feel these maladaptive and negative emotions to such an extent that we have long-term problems with our lives. The main reason we feel these emotions is illustrated by the cartoon figure of a 'saint'.

Show OHT 9

Figure 5.5. The saint and the checklist. ('Saint' by V. Parslow-Stafford. 'Checklist' by R. Allen. Halo and thought bubble from IMSI's MasterClips Collection, 1895 Francisco Blvd. East, San Rafael, CA 94901-5506, USA)

The figure of a 'saint' represents the absolute values we have for ourselves and each other. The most common beliefs which occur at point 'B' in the A-B-C sequence are 'I must be perfect'; or 'I must be a perfect mother (father, worker, etc.) to be any good'; 'everybody must like me for me to be any good'; or 'other people must behave perfectly'. That is, we set saint-like standards for ourselves and others. If we do not come up to our own standards we conclude that we are worthless, or no good, and get depressed. If we worry, or *fear* we won't come up to our own standards or those of others we become anxious; and if other people don't come up to our standards, we become angry.

We have a sort of checklist in our heads for 'sainthood'. Only if we (or others) fulfil all our standards do we consider that we (or the others) are worth while.

The problem of course is that we cannot all be saints. By setting such high standards, and insisting that we must achieve them *all*, we set ourselves up to be non-saints. Since we believe that only saints are worth while, we then become worthless in our own eyes.

This is a very simple presentation of how we come to feel those negative emotions, but we will talk about it in greater detail next week.

Some of you may be thinking 'what's wrong with high standards?' and of course there is nothing wrong with high standards. What's wrong is that you say 'I am no good' *because* you don't reach those high standards.

The suitcase analogy

Show OHT 10 or drawing of the suitcase analogy, Figure 5.6. Use the following to explain the steps in Cognitive Therapy.

Now, before the end of this session, we're going to talk a bit about how cognitive therapy works. You might think of your mind as being like a suitcase that you've carried with you on your travels in life. Over your travels you will have collected all sorts of bits and pieces, which are your attitudes and beliefs. Some of them were useful at the time, some of them were given to you (often by your parents or by significant figures in your life),

Figure 5.6 The suitcase analogy for the process of cognitive therapy. ('Suitcase by R. Allen)

some were cheap, and some were attractive, so you put them in your suitcase. Now, these beliefs are making that suitcase too heavy to carry around, that is they are causing you to feel the pain of negative emotion.

What we are going to do in this cognitive therapy program is to open that suitcase, and see what is inside. We are going to examine each item or belief and decide whether it is worth keeping, whether it is true or untrue, whether it is useful to you or not. Then we are going to teach you how to take all the unwanted beliefs and take them to the dump, or get rid of them.

So the step we've done today could be called 'finding the combination', because the A-B-C sequence is the key to unlocking your mind. Another part of the first step is looking at the things in the top of your suitcase, and overcoming any resistance you might have to going any further. The next stage is concerned with discovering what other thoughts you have which may be causing emotional problems. This is like unpacking the suitcase.

The next step is doing a stock-take: listing and organising the contents of the suitcase so you can make sensible decisions about what to throw away and what to keep. We make lists of your beliefs, draw up cognitive maps of how they relate to each other, and organise them into categories. This is something like putting the contents of your suit-case into piles, and then making lists of them.

The fourth step is like weighing the things you've taken out of the suitcase and decid-ing whether you want and/or need to carry them around. Of course you might use all sorts of criteria for keeping things in your suitcase, but the main criterion we use with your beliefs is whether they are true or false. In this step we use five different ways of challenging the beliefs you have obtained in the previous steps.

Once you have decided what you are going to get rid of, you want to take it to the dump. This is not always easy with beliefs, just as it might be difficult for you to get a lot of rubbish to the dump at one time. We teach you five main ways of taking beliefs to the dump, and we also look at ways in which you can prevent yourself from collecting garbage in the future.

So that is the process. As I have said, homework is part of it. We have started to find out your beliefs using the A-B-C sequence. You should continue to do that during the rest of the week.

As part of your homework this week, I would like you to collect the worst A-B-C sequence that happens to you each day, and the ten worst things which have happened to you in adult life and write them down in A-B-C sequence, but before that we have an exercise.

You may wish to demonstrate putting events from the past into the three column format. You may wish to distinguish between thoughts they might have had at the time, and their current reaction to remembering the event.

EXERCISE: GUIDED IMAGERY

I want everyone to get as comfortable as you can on those chairs. Just ease up and relax as much as you can, because we're going to do an imagery exercise. The more relaxed you are the better your imagination will work. Now close your eyes and imagine you are lying on a beautiful beach. The sand is nicely moulded to the shape of your body so you can lie there in total relaxation. The sun is pleasantly warm on your skin. You can smell the salt smell of the sea, and you can hear the soft swishing of the waves. You can hear a seagull from time to time ... there is the beautiful smell of tropical flowers ... Or you can imagine yourself strolling through the most beautiful garden ever. You are strolling slowly through roses, rhododendrons and other beautiful flowers. It is early morning, there is dew on the grass and a soft dampness in the air. You hear the song of birds. You pick a rose and smell its exquisite perfume ... Or you can imagine a pleasant scene of your own choosing. Just take a few moments to do that now. Build it up from you memory or your imagination until you have a clear picture, then add the sounds ... the smells ... the sensations on your skin. Just take a few moments to do that now, until I tell you to stop.

OK. Now open your eyes and come back to the real world. What did you feel in response to the pleasant scenery?

Draw the parallel between the guided imagery and thinking pleasant thoughts and the pleasant emotional consequences of doing both.

SUMMARY

To summarise today's session, we have looked at how thinking, doing, and our body processes are linked up. We have seen how the way people think affects the way they feel, and we have seen how just imagining pleasant scenery can make us feel relaxed. How many of you think that your problems could be due to your thoughts or beliefs?

Just note the numbers without comment. You may wish to take note of the people who said no and repeat the question after a few more sessions.

HOMEWORK FOR SESSION ONE

1. Write down the 10 worst things in adult life using the A-B-C sequence.
2. Write down the worst A-B-C sequence that you have each day.

   Check for any questions.

PROBLEMS THAT MAY ARISE IN SESSION ONE

There are number of major problems which may arise in the first session. In the first instance, people may not be able to access their thoughts in order to write them down. I have found this mostly with older people or very practically oriented people. For such people it is possible that cognitive therapy of the kind described here may not be the easiest treatment to deliver. If it is necessary to persist, then a process of shaping by successive approximations may be useful. You can start by helping such people to access problem solving thinking, then their opinions and attitudes, and then their spontaneous thoughts in situations with low emotional impact such as everyday events. I have found it useful to have them discuss the thoughts they had in the waiting room before they came to the session.

Some people may have difficulty with accepting the three systems model. It may be useful to provide or elicit from the client further examples of processes in one system influencing the other ... the effect of alcohol on confidence, for example. If you have any psychophysiological recording devices you can demonstrate the effect of positive and negative imagery on heart rate, skin conductance and other psychophysiological measures.

One reason for the three-systems model is to provide an integrated explanation that allows for a number of approaches to depression. About one third of the depressed people who have been through the program have also been receiving medication. The program itself was developed within a community mental health service in which patients might be receiving three or even more forms of therapy.

For the people who have difficulty accepting responsibility for their depression it may be necessary to address this issue directly, perhaps in one or more individual sessions. These people will often present it as a question of the value of continuing in the group because they see their depression as a biological problem. My approach is to consider the problem as a choice exercise about whether it is worth their while continuing in the group, almost a 'what have you got to lose?' approach. I tend to analyse the question as a series of pros and cons and leave the client to make the decision. I think it is important not to oversell the group.

In my experience it is not essential for group participants to have total acceptance of the cognitive model of depression at this stage. For people who are doubtful I try to promote their keeping an open mind. Most people who continue in the groups seem to accept the model within a few sessions. It is uncertain how critical this is in the process of recovery, and future research should consider this question.

Other problems that occur in this session are more technical in nature, and are mostly to do with putting the right things in the right columns. Provision of corrective feedback is usually sufficient, but in some cases it may be necessary to provide additional explanation as to what an emotion is and what a thought is and the difference between them. I usually try to get people to limit the emotion words to the most basic and specific emotions of fear/anxiety, sad/depressed, angry, guilty, rather than 'upset', or 'outraged'.

Chapter 6

THERAPY SESSION TWO

GOALS OF SESSION TWO

1. For participants to obtain knowledge of the following:
   - the main aspects of the cognitive theories of depression, anxiety, and anger;
   - the characteristics of automatic thoughts and how to catch them;
   - the main cognitive distortions or logical errors and be able to recognise them in their own thinking.
2. For participants to acknowledge potential resistances they may have to have cognitive therapy and develop strategies to counter the resistances.

SUMMARY OF SESSION TWO

- Review of homework from previous session
- Lecture A: Cognitive theory of depression
- Exercise: Categorising beliefs
- Lecture B: Anxiety and pathological anger; catching automatic thoughts
- Exercise: Automatic thoughts associated with group therapy
- Lecture C: Resistances to therapy
- Exercise: Identifying potential resistances and strategies for prevention
- Homework for next week

REVIEW OF HOMEWORK FROM SESSION ONE

Check the worst things in adult life and first seven worst daily A-B-Cs. Make sure that people have discriminated between events, thoughts and emotions and correct/ explain where necessary.

LECTURE A

Theory of emotional disturbance

Last session I presented you with the idea that your thoughts about an event or situation determine your feelings about that event or situation. This week I am going to talk about how the way we think causes the emotional problems of depression and anxiety.

Scientists have many theories about what causes depression. You will remember that last week I talked about the three interlinked systems that make up a person: thoughts, physiological processes and behaviour.

Some groups of scientists say that depression is caused by things going wrong in one system and some say it is caused by things going wrong in another.

- Some say that depression is caused by malfunction of the system of chemicals that carry messages from one nerve to another.
- Some say that depression occurs because a person does not have enough pleasant things happening to him or her.
- And some say that people become depressed because of a faulty thinking style.

There are treatments based on all these theories of depression:

- Antidepressant medications are supposed to correct chemical malfunction.
- One particular system of therapy gets people to increase the number of pleasant events they experience.
- And another system of therapy teaches people to change their faulty ways of thinking. This is the therapy we will be using in this group.

With the exception of a small group of very depressed people, we don't know which people benefit from which kind of treatment, so the treatment you get depends on which therapist you go to. Medical practitioners will usually prescribe antidepressant medication, which is of course a treatment acting on the physiological system, and psychologists will design either a treatment which attempts to change your thinking, or one that attempts to change your behaviour. If you are lucky you will get them all, but most people only get medication.

With depression we don't just consider what causes, or starts the depression. We also need to consider what keeps the depression going. Even if depression started off as chemical malfunction, it could be kept going by faulty thinking, or the other way around. As I have indicated, we believe that all of the three systems are interlinked and that for this reason it doesn't matter which system is used for treatment. There is plenty of evidence that intervening in the thinking system is effective in treating most people with depression.

Let's now look at how thinking patterns can cause depression. Some people who are depressed seem to think about things in different ways from people who are not depressed. We think that these people always think this way, but we're not sure where the thinking style comes from, either. People may be born with it, or they may learn it from their parents.

There are four ways in which a person's thinking style may be faulty.

- They may have *negative automatic thoughts.*
- They may have negative or absolutistic *core beliefs.*
- Their thoughts may have negative *content* about themselves, the world, and the future.
- They may make a number of *logical errors* in the way they think.

We are going to talk about these in turn.

Automatic thoughts

You will remember that last session I talked about the thoughts, or beliefs, that came at 'B' in the A-B-C sequence of activating event, belief, and emotional consequence. Very often the belief at 'B' is automatic. This program is based very much on the work of Dr

Aaron Beck and his view of depression. Dr Beck defined the characteristics of automatic thoughts as follows.

Show OHTs 11 & 12

1. They are short and specific. They occur extremely rapidly, immediately after the event.
2. They do not occur in sentences, but may consist of a few key words or images.
3. They do not arise from careful thought.
4. They do not occur in a logical series of steps such as in problem solving.
5. They seem to happen just by reflex.
6. You do not summon them up, and you can't send them away.
7. They seem reasonable at the time.
8. The words of the thought may differ, but often a person will have automatic thoughts with the same theme, e.g. that she is a failure, worthless, etc.
9. People with the same emotional problem have the same kind of automatic thoughts.
10. Automatic thoughts have more distortion of reality than other types of thinking.

(Adapted from Beck *et al.*, 1979)

So what happens is that people have a number of habitual negative automatic thoughts that they repeat to themselves in similar situations, such as when they are unsuccessful at completing a task. Each time they repeat these thoughts the emotion builds up more and more. If you told a football team to run round the oval chanting 'we're no good, we're a bunch of losers', you wouldn't expect them to play well, would you? Or if your best friend told you a hundred times a day that you are a failure, you'd certainly feel bad then. Well of course the same thing happens if you repeat those messages to yourself … even if you don't believe them in the first place, they come to affect you more and more.

The same thing happens with anxiety, when people keep telling themselves how horrible, or dangerous a certain event will be. They then get more and more apprehensive and frightened of that thing happening. In this way people often get very frightened about going mad, being rejected by their friends, being alone, or becoming ill.

People can also have automatic thoughts which lead to anger, by telling themselves hundreds of times a day that someone has no right to behave in such and such a way, or should have done things x, y and z, or should not have done things p, q and r. Depressed people often become angry with themselves in this way. I suspect many marriages break up because of brooding resentment, which builds up through negative automatic thoughts.

Negative core beliefs

The second way in which a thinking style can be faulty is through negative core beliefs, otherwise known as schemas. While automatic thoughts are often specific to a situation, core beliefs are much more general, and reflect a person's overall attitude to life. Schemas may be conclusions you've reached about the world, attitudes taught to you by your parents, or related to choices that you have made yourself. Examples might be 'winning is everything'; 'it is necessary to be physically attractive to be liked by others'; 'only an incompetent parent hits children'. Automatic thoughts are the product of schemas.

Psychologists have come to recognise the most frequently encountered of these core beliefs, and here is a list of the main types of negative schemas people with emotional problems tend to have.

Show OHTs 13 & 14, or hand out a list of common negative schemas.

I Stink*	I am worthless, no good, of no value.
You Stink*	A person who offends me is no good, a total bastard.
Namby-Pamby*	I can't stand it, I can't cope, I'll go crazy.
Monster*	I am coming to harm, I am sick.
Doomsday*	This event is catastrophic, the future is hopeless.
Fairy-tale*	Things should be better; the world should be like x.
Alone	I am rejected, I am alone.
Kitten	I am powerless.
Bomb	I am out of control.
Victim	The world/fate/God/the cosmos is unfair, has done me wrong.

Figure 6.1. Common negative core beliefs or schemas

The above list of negative beliefs has been derived from a number of sources, predominantly from Ellis' list of ten major irrational beliefs, and from McMullin & Casey's 'Thoughts which cause problems'. The labels that are asterisked above come from McMullin and Casey (1977).

These beliefs can be held in three different ways, which may in fact reflect three different levels of activation of the same schema. They may be absolute, as expressed above, they may be predicted, as in 'I will be worthless,' 'I will go mad'; or they may be conditional, as in 'If I fail to achieve I will be worthless'; 'If my partner was to leave me, I would end up alone'.

Negative content: The negative cognitive triad

The third way in which a thinking style can be faulty is when a person has a negative view of themselves, the world, and the future. That is, they come to think that they are a bad person, that the world is a bad place, and that things will continue to go badly.

A similar idea is presented in the learned helplessness and hopelessness models of depression, developed by Abramson and colleagues (Abramson, Seligman and Teasdale, 1978; Abramson, Metalsky, and Alloy, 1989). In the hopelessness model, a person comes to believe that bad things happen because of unchangeable circumstances with global effects on their lives. The person then becomes helpless, hopeless, and depressed. It is possible that people learn to think this way because of a lot of bad experiences as children.

All of the three kinds of negative thinking I have described can be analysed to discover whether they are true or false, and that is one of the things that we will be doing in this course. We shall be catching your automatic thoughts, discovering your core beliefs, and finding out about your view of yourself, the world and the future. We will be considering these things very carefully. If any of these kinds of thinking is causing your depression, then that thinking is probably wrong, and can be changed. Since that thinking has probably been maintaining your depression, changing it is likely to lead to improved mood, and improved ability to cope with depression in the future.

Logical errors

The fourth faulty kind of thinking, making *logical errors*, is concerned with the *process* of thinking. Logic is the reasoning process that you use when you draw conclusions from the events around you.

Show OHT 15, 16, 17, 18 as appropriate.

There are two major kinds of logical error: *extreme thinking,* and *arbitrary thinking*. Extreme thinking is when there is some distortion in the process of thinking, usually an exaggeration or minimisation of some kind. In arbitrary thinking the conclusion or inference is made without any process at all.

Extreme thinking is broken down into four kinds: going beyond the facts, misinterpreting the facts, not considering all the facts, and using dichotomous categories for things which are really continuous and rating things that are unrateable

(a) **Going beyond the facts** is when the person makes a conclusion that is not justified by the facts. There are five ways you can do this.

When you conclude a situation is **more dire than justified** you conclude a situation is worse than it really is. People do this frequently: for example concluding that one small mistake will cause them to lose their job.

In **false absolutes** you use absolute words such as 'never', 'always', 'everyone', and 'everything' when they are not justified. For example: 'I am never any good at anything' or 'everyone hates me'.

In **faulty prediction** you predict that things will turn out worse than is truly likely. This can be combined with other logical errors, as in 'I will never be any good' (absolutism in the future), and 'My project will fail' (more dire than justified in the future).

Invalid allocation of responsibility involves allocating disproportionate amounts of responsibility for negative events onto either yourself or a significant other person.

Unjustified conclusions about motive or opinion is concluding you know the reason for a person's behaviour, or you know their opinion, when you do not have access to the full set of their reasons, drives, and motives. An example is concluding that someone is treating you indifferently because he or she dislikes you. There could of course be many other reasons: he or she is distracted, is worred about something else, or has a headache.

(b) People **misinterpreting the facts** see only one conclusion from a set of facts. For example, a person sees a car outside a lover's house and concludes that it is the rival. Facts may also be misinterpreted because the interpretation is biased. A depressed person will see all events as being negatively related to him or her.

(c) In **failing to consider all the facts,** a person may just ignore facts that detract from the negative conclusion they are coming to, such as ignoring all the times they have been successful when they are concluding that they are hopeless.

(d) **Using dichotomous categories for continuous phenomena** refers to making judgements about oneself or others. You judge people as either totally in one category, such as a 'good' referee, or totally in another, such as a 'hopeless' referee, when a continuum is much more reasonable. A similar phenomenon is **rating things that are essentially unrateable,** such as people.

There are two kinds of **Arbitrary thinking**: *shoulds,* and *using emotion to verify belief.* In **shoulds,** statements of desire ('I would like to go for a swim'; 'We would all prefer that people do not steal from us') are changed into baseless imperatives: 'I should go for a swim'; 'he/she should not steal'.

In **using emotion to verify belief** a person claims that a conclusion is right because it 'feels' right. This is a logical error because emotions by themselves do not contain any information that could verify a belief.

Making logical errors is important in two parts of the process of developing emotional difficulties: in the events in childhood that lead a person to develop a negative schema, and when a schema is activated after a critical incident.

EXERCISE: CATEGORISING BELIEFS AND THOUGHT PROCESSES

For the beliefs you got in the A-B-Cs you collected last week, try to decide which kind of belief or faulty thought process they exemplify.

Walk round group and coach them if necessary to identify which of the ten main schemas or ten logical errors the beliefs they have got so far exemplify.

LECTURE B

Anxiety

I have spent a fair amount of time talking about the way in which faulty thinking causes depression. Depression is not the only emotional problem people suffer from, and I know that many of you suffer from anxiety problems.

Faulty thinking causes anxiety in much the same way as it causes depression. I said last time that anxiety occurs when the thoughts are about danger, or harm, coming to you or people and things you value. So we would expect that automatic thoughts about danger could lead to increased anxiety. There is no depressive triad in anxiety, but cognitive distortions or logical errors can occur. This is how it works.

When a person decides that a situation is dangerous, the person then tries to work out:

1. how likely it is that the harmful event will occur;
2. how soon it will occur;
3. how much damage there will be;
4. what can be done to avoid the harm.

You can see that it would be very easy to make an error in any of these four steps. Anxious people do just that: they exaggerate the likelihood of harm, they exaggerate how bad the damage will be, they under-rate their abilities to avoid harm, and they tend to overestimate how much external events relate to them. The most common logical error in anxious people is to decide that some unpleasant event, such as a panic attack, is absolutely awful, and likely to lead to their death or insanity, and to spend most of their days worrying about the possibility of the unpleasant event. The anxiety they generate by worrying in this way is often worse than the unpleasant event itself would have been.

In addition anxious people are very attuned to events inside their bodies. They'll notice a change in heartbeat and then start the process I have just discussed: 'that change in heartbeat means I'll have a heart attack and die' and so on.

The other thing which happens with anxiety is that more and more things become associated with danger, so the person becomes anxious more and more of the time.

With anxiety, as with depression, it is important to identify the automatic thoughts and to reduce how often they occur, and to challenge the cognitive distortions and to learn to think logically and objectively. The first step in this process is to 'catch' the automatic thoughts.

Thought catching

Show OHT 19

Here is a little analogy that I hope will be useful in understanding how to identify automatic thoughts.

Catching your automatic thoughts, or ATs, is like hunting a very shy animal, capturing it alive, and taking it back to a zoo to be tamed. First of all you need to know what the animal looks like. Well I've told you that in the list of their characteristics. Let's run through them again. (*Do so*) Next we have to find out about the AT's habits. We can look for its tracks or droppings. With automatic thoughts we can tell where they've been by the emotion they leave behind ... a stab of anxiety, a brief sinking feeling, a flash of anger. Be on the look out for those signs and see if you can catch a glimpse of the automatic thoughts. As you get used to it you will be able to see more of the AT, until you are able to write it down in a complete sentence.

Another thing you can do is to study the habits of the ATs. See what time of day they come out, and in what circumstances. You can then be waiting next day, or next time you are in a similar situation. You may find it easier to capture the AT that way.

Or you can set traps for the AT. You can set up a situation in which you think they are likely to occur. If parties make you anxious, plan to go to one, and see what ATs you get. If doing the budget makes you depressed, do it, but be on the lookout for ATs. If you have a good imagination, you can trick the ATs, by imagining the sort of situations they are known to frequent.

Once you have the automatic thoughts you can put them into the ABC format we talked about last week.

So in summary:

1. Know the characteristics of automatic thoughts.
2. Look for their tracks, i.e. the emotion they leave behind.
3. Know their habits and be on the lookout.
4. Set traps.
5. Trick them with your imagination.

Figure 6.2. An automatic thought?

EXERCISE: AUTOMATIC THOUGHTS ABOUT GROUP THERAPY

Have participants write down and share with the group what they remember as their first automatic thoughts about the therapy when they entered the room for the first time. If necessary have them rehearse the scene, and/or use any emotions described as a cue to the automatic thought they might have. Or use some of the techniques in the 'shy animal' analogy (OHT 19).

LECTURE C: RESISTANCES TO THERAPY

We have now got through most of the preliminary material, and we're about to move on to the hard work. This is a good time to discuss resistance.

There are a large number of ways in which people consciously or unconsciously do things which reduce the effectiveness of therapy, or make it harder for the therapy to work. The single main one is not doing the homework. It is not possible to complete this program without doing substantial work at home. Homework can also be done half-heartedly. Perversely, some people will not try their hardest becase somehow failure is not so great if you weren't trying in the first place! What can happen with homework is that you gradually fall behind, or you miss one session, and then think that you are too far behind to catch up. Part of the service we offer is that we will help you out of session time if you miss a session, or are having difficulty, but sometimes people don't use this help.

Probably the other main resistance is not keeping an open mind about cognitive therapy. If you have a strong view that cognitive therapy can't help you, then you will spend more time arguing with what I say in your head than trying to apply what I'm saying to your own satisfaction.

McMullin and Giles (1981) recognise three other common 'sabotages': trying to deal with all your problems at once, denying improvement when it occurs, and refusing to keep trying. I'm sure there are lots of others, and you may even come up with some new ones!

Of course resistance to therapy can itself be based on negative or irrational beliefs. Can you think of some beliefs people might have which might prevent them from carrying out the tasks of therapy? Or that would prevent them from benefiting as much as possible from therapy?

EXERCISE

Identifying potential resistance

Divide people into groups of three and have them:

1. decide how they would resist therapy if they were going to;
2. develop strategies to counter resistance;
3. report back (if time available).

Homework contract

As many of you have noted, the main way in which people resist therapy is not doing the homework, and while you might be really keen now, it's important that you keep up the amount of work you do. For this reason I am suggesting that you make up a home-work contract for yourself. I will hand out a form to you, but you are welcome to devise your own. I suggest you specify now exactly when you are going to do your homework. Allow about five hours each week, and it is best if there is a clear signal before the time you have set aside: for example the finish of the TV news, or after your children have gone to school. If you get yourself into a routine now, that routine will keep you going right through the course and beyond. As suggested on the form, you may wish to reward yourself each week for sticking to your homework schedule. This may sound silly, but it does work!

> *Hand out and have them fill out the homework contract (Appendix 5) unless they object.*

HOMEWORK FOR SESSION TWO

1. Capture as many automatic thoughts as possible. Record them in the A-B-C format, if you can. Try to get at least one per day.
2. Finish belief categorisation and drawing up the contract.
3. Continue to note your worst A-B-C event each day.

PROBLEMS THAT MAY ARISE IN SESSION TWO

There are few problems associated with the Lecture A material in this session. If people are having difficulties with the theory then it may help to explain it in more detail using examples relevant to the person.

The second half of the session is probably more important. The biggest problem is that often people do not have insight into the form that their resistance might take. In these circumstances it may help for the therapist to identify likely forms of resistance for particular individuals and to gently guide those individuals towards identifying those forms of resistance themselves. The therapist can guide the participant towards adopting a suitable strategy to counter that resistance. Examples of the kinds of resistances can be found in Beck *et al.* (1979). I have not had many difficulties with overt resistance of the kind mentioned by Beck *et al.*, apart from those mentioned with respect to Session 1. The main problem I have encountered is of people dropping out of therapy without explanation. This may be offset to some degree by a permissive attitude towards people who are not completing the homework, which may of course have negative consequences. Under these circumstances we can hope that people get enough out of the material within the session to make some progress. I shall present some information in the last chapter of this book that suggests that clinically significant effects can be achieved without any homework.

Chapter 7

THERAPY SESSION THREE

GOALS OF SESSION THREE

1. To orient participants to the idea that their thoughts have behavioural consequences as well as emotional consequences, and to the idea that those behavioural consequences may themselves be dysfunctional.
2. To teach participants about the nature of schemas (core beliefs, schemata, dysfunctional attitudes) and about the relationship between schemas and automatic thoughts, and to teach them to identify the schemas using the vertical arrow method (Burns, 1980).

SUMMARY OF SESSION THREE

- Review of homework from previous session
- Lecture A: Thought injection
- Exercise: Thought injection
- Lecture B: Introduction to the vertical arrow procedure
- Exercise: Vertical arrow
- Homework for next week

REVIEW OF HOMEWORK FROM SESSION TWO

1. Material on automatic thoughts, success in catching automatic thoughts;
2. writing down the worst A-B-C situation they've had each day;
3. any questions from the reading material;
4. review material on resistance.

> As for the previous session, check that A-B-Cs have been recorded validly: that the beliefs column contains testable sentences, that emotions are confined to the C column, and that the C column does not contain cognitive material.

The next section is an exercise, designed essentially to have participants accept the idea that particular thoughts lead to particular emotions, and to negative self-defeating behaviour.

LECTURE A: BEHAVIOURAL CONSEQUENCES OF BELIEFS

Over the past two sessions I have introduced you to the A-B-C concept, in which automatic thoughts or beliefs at 'B' are associated with emotional consequences at 'C'. There are also *behavioural* consequences of each thought or belief, and that is what we are going to consider now.

Let's look at that list of beliefs that we introduced last session.

Show OHT 13.

Imagine that a person had the belief 'I'm worthless', 'I'm no good', or 'I stink'. We saw in the first session that their emotional consequence would probably be depression. How might a person behave who thought they were worthless?

Coach participants to generate examples such as self-effacing behaviour, not standing up for themselves, even suicidal behaviour.

We also saw in the last session that beliefs could be conditional. How might a person behave who had the belief 'I must be perfect to be worth while'?

Coach participants to describe obsessively perfectionistic behaviour, such as meticulous house cleaning. Then use some other examples, such as 'I am worthless unless I am loved, liked by everybody', 'I am worthless unless I am the best in my sport, profession, activity'. When they have the idea, proceed to the exercise.

EXERCISE: THOUGHT INJECTION

For the exercise, I would like you to go through that process for all the beliefs on the list, first for the absolute belief, and then for at least one conditional belief. Let's imagine that we can inject the belief into the mind of someone walking by outside. If a person had that belief really strongly, how would they feel? How would they behave?

Split participants into small groups of 2 or 3 and have them discuss and write down how each of the other beliefs might affect the feelings and behaviour of someone who had them injected into his or her mind. Use the list of beliefs from the previous chapter (OHTs 13 and 14).

LECTURE B: THE VERTICAL (OR DOWNWARD) ARROW PROCEDURE

We have now been talking about A-B-Cs or the *combination* to the suitcase for several sessions. It is now time to start *unpacking* the suitcase, and we do that by means of the vertical arrow technique. This procedure was first described by David Burns in his 1980 book: *Feeling Good: The New Mood Therapy*, and has since been adopted by other leading practitioners of cognitive therapy.

First, let's consider some more how your thinking works. You have now had some practice at catching *automatic thoughts*, the surface thoughts, and have been writing them down so that you can see the patterns that occur. You may have found that one or two sorts of automatic thoughts seem to be repeated in certain circumstances, lead to particular emotions, and occur over and over during a typical day. Have any of you found these things?

Elicit examples from the group.

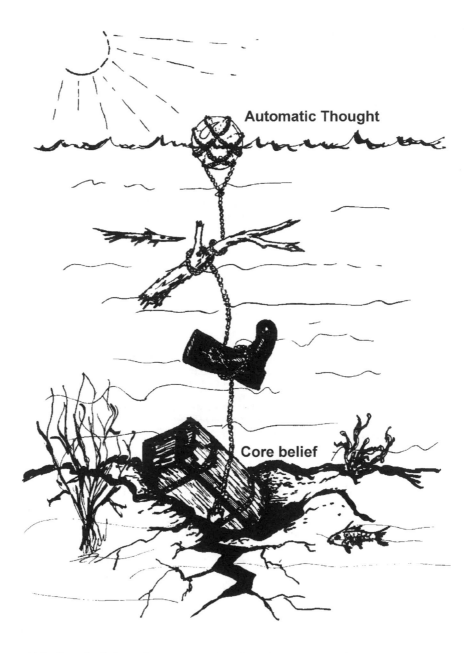

Figure 7.1. Core beliefs and automatic thoughts: the ocean analogy. ('Ocean Analogy' by V. Parslow-Stafford)

Sometimes it will be obvious why these automatic thoughts cause the emotion that comes after them. Other times it will not.

Show OHT 20.

Your mind could be compared to the ocean. Automatic thoughts are things that bob up to the surface. In cases where the connection between the automatic thought and the emotion is not immediately obvious, it is necessary to go below the surface, to go deeper into your mind, to discover your negative core beliefs or schemas.

Sometimes when you are daydreaming, or when you are in bed just waiting to go to sleep, your mind will just run on. It will think about one thing, and then pass on to something very different from where you started. It's a bit like a domino snake in which one domino knocks over another, then another, till the domino at the end is set off. Does this sort of thinking happen to you?

You could demonstrate with a domino snake!

The link that connects one thought to another is usually *association*, a connection between the meaning of one thought and the meaning of the other. We need to identify the automatic thought or surface belief, then follow the associations down to discover the core belief. We should also note that the logical errors we mentioned in Session 2 often occur in the connection between one thought and the next, too.

Another way to think of it is that your brain is like a vast network of coloured light-bulbs joined by wires. If you switch one on, another will soon start flashing, then another, and so on.

Draw this, or show OHT 21 as below.

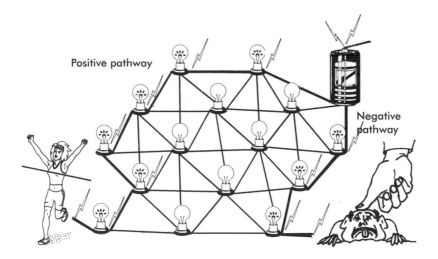

Figure 7.2. The bulb-net analogy: the associations can follow different paths in your head. ('Winner' and 'Thumb' by V. Parslow-Stafford. Other elements from IMSI's MasterClips collection, 1895 Francisco Blvd East, San Rafael, CA 94901-5506, USA)

Sometimes these sequences can become like habits: in similar situations you always think through the same sequence of thoughts, as if there is a well-worn pathway through your beliefs. The thought that causes the emotion is not the one you started with, but the one at the end of the chain. In the picture you can see there are two pathways. In one the path leads to a core belief associated with winning, the other with being put down! These thoughts at the end of the pathway are called 'core beliefs', 'dysfunctional assumptions', 'rules' or 'schemas'. They are usually more general than automatic thoughts and can be recognised by their absolute, definite or imperative sound. They often start 'I (you, one, he, she, it) must, should', 'I can't', 'Never', 'Everyone'. They may be things which you have worked out in your lifetime, and which you no longer question, such as 'you can't trust anyone' or 'you should trust everyone' to give two conflicting examples. The list of negative beliefs we used in the exercise earlier is a list of common core beliefs that are often found at the end of people's pathways of association.

In sequences of thoughts that lead to depression, there is a tendency for the association to be always negative, so that the chain eventually connects with a core belief that is strongly associated with negative emotion.

To understand the reasons for your emotions, we have to trace the habitual connections between your thoughts, and to try to find out your core beliefs. There is just one thing that determines which thought is associated with which, and that is the *meaning* that is associated with the beliefs. Meaning comes from inside us, and we apply it to anything we sense from the outside world, and also to things that we experience inside our bodies. So for every situation or event or item we observe there are the objective facts, and there is the *meaning* we attach to those objective facts. Meaning goes beyond the objective facts. For example the sign for 'no smoking' could be described as a picture of a cigarette with a diagonal line across it, but we know that the meaning of that is 'no smoking'.

Human beings have a tendency to attach meaning to every single event or item they are aware of, and then to associate something else with the first meaning, and so on. If people hear a siren they think of fire, crime or injury. One person might hear a siren and think 'Fire! I wonder if I turned the stove off. I haven't turned it on... I haven't done anything about dinner... what will I have for dinner?...' We are also particularly sensitive to the behaviour of others. Intonation of voice, or a smile, or even a twitch of the mouth, is always given some meaning. And different events have different meaning for different people. A smell, or a piece of music, will be associated with happy times for one person, sad times for another.

And where does the meaning come from? Well it comes from at least three sources: what we learn from our culture, what we learn for ourselves, and our own choices. Most of us will not have experienced the horror of Nazi Germany, but the swastika is still a symbol of evil to us. A child may learn that the only way she can please her mother is by doing extremely well at schoolwork, so in later life, any failure comes to mean rejection. Such a person may continue to have a high need to achieve perfection long after it is important to please her mother. Another person may choose not to smack his children because he doesn't want to be like his parents who beat him violently. Having to smack his children then comes to mean to him that he is a violent child beater.

The next thing we are going to do is one of the most important parts of therapy. Each of you needs to find out:

- What are your habitual chains of association?
- What are your core beliefs?
- What are your typical logical errors?

You do this by following the association process slowly:

1. by taking each A-B-C sequence one at a time;
2. by focusing on the emotion and the first automatic thought;
3. by assuming the particular automatic thought is true;
4.   and by asking yourself three questions:

If that was true…
- what would it/does it mean to me?
- why would it be/is it so upsetting?
- why would it be/is it so bad?

The technique is called the 'vertical arrow', and this is how you do it. We use the short downward arrow between the statements to remind us that we are following the chain of your negative associations downward from the surface to your core belief. OHT 22 (Figure 7.3) shows an example for a footballer whose team lost a game in which he failed a particular attempt to kick a goal. Notice how the beliefs become more general and absolute as we go through the procedure. We can also assume that the emotional intensity also increases as we go down the vertical arrow.

Figure 7.3. Footballer vertical arrow. ('Footballer' by V. Parslow-Stafford)

The next OHT (OHT 23, Figure 7.4) contains another example. In this example the activating event is a blast on the referee's whistle, which the experiencer is interpreting as being inappropriate. Again the statements become more general and the emotion probably more intense as they work down the vertical arrow. The core belief on this occasion is the one we've come to know as 'you stink'. Finally, the next OHT shows a more extended naturalistic vertical arrow.

Show OHTs 24 and 25.

DEMONSTRATION

Ask for a volunteer to provide an example of an A-B-C, then do a vertical arrow for their A-B-C, demonstrating the questions. Depending upon available time, you may wish to do a second demonstration.

That wasn't a foul!

⬇

That ref is biased!

⬇

He shouldn't be reffing

⬇

He's hopeless!

Figure 7.4. Referee vertical arrow. ('Referee' by V. Parslow-Stafford)

A: Doing the housework

C: Anxious

B1 I want everything to be spotless otherwise people will think I'm dirty
and untidy

↓

B2 People woould think badly of me

↓

B3 I will be unwanted and neglected

↓

B4 I am useless and a nobody

↓

B5 Nobody will want to love me

↓

B6 I will always be alone

↓

B7 I am unwanted

↓

B8 I will always be unhappy

Figure 7.5. Housework vertical arrow

EXERCISE: VERTICAL ARROW

Have the participants do a vertical arrow with one of their own A-B-Cs. Therapists walk around the room and coach participants. Help people if they are stuck by taking them through one cycle and then leave them to conduct the next cycle themselves, with prompting if necessary. OHT 25 is the set of instructions to follow. It can be put up for the participants' guidance.

1. Follow the negative associations by asking the questions
   'If ——— is true, what would that mean to me?' or
   'If ——— is true, why would that be so bad?'
2. Concentrate on one emotion at a time.
3. Search for core meaning of statements.
5. Avoid descriptions of feeling.
6. Avoid questions 'Why is he/she ...'.
7. Avoid statements of desire 'I wish ...'.

Figure 7.6. Basic instructions for vertical arrow procedure.

Show OHT 25.

This is probably the most difficult part of the program, for both the participants and the group leader. It is important that the group leader has extensive experience at doing vertical arrows with individual patients. The best advice is for the group leader to be very aware of all the approaches and hints for doing the vertical arrow, contained in this session and the next one. Probably the most important things to remember are to focus on key words, and to try to keep the emotion you are tracking the same. It is also important to avoid getting descriptions of emotion, as in 'I would feel depressed and miserable' as items in the vertical arrow, since that usually leads to circularity. If the vertical arrow is going well, you should be aware of facial or postural cues of increasing emotional intensity. By the same token do not be concerned about a little circularity. Sometimes it is useful just to explore what comes during the process rather than trying to push it in a certain direction.

HOMEWORK FOR SESSION THREE

1. Continue to write out A-B-Cs, especially for new situations.
2. Complete thought injection.
3. Write the behavioural Consequences (bCs) for the A-B-Cs completed so far.
4. Do two vertical arrow analyses on their own A-B-Cs.

PROBLEMS THAT MAY ARISE IN SESSION THREE

Few problems arise from the thought injection exercise, although some people have difficulty grasping the idea of a thought being injected. For these people it may be necessary simply to bypass the concept and say, 'Well, what if this person had that thought, what would he or she do?'

In any event the thought injection material is not used further in the program, although it might be useful in any associated individual therapy which is being conducted.

On the other hand teaching participants to do their own vertical arrows is quite diffi-cult. Two main kinds of problems can occur. Some people will just get stuck, and other people will tend to either go round in circles, or will simply go off track, generating beliefs that have less and less relationship to the original. A good vertical arrow is one that has the following characteristics:

- The statements are clearly related to each other.
- The same emotion is involved for all statements.
- The statements are more general as one goes down the vertical arrow.
- The statements become more emotionally evocative as one goes down the vertical arrow.

For those that get stuck I try to explore the meaning of the statement they have by asking questions which help me to understand the meaning of the statement to them. This can be by exploring the meaning, to them, of the words they use, e.g. 'So what is a "loser" ', 'If you were like that what would the consequences be?' At times it may be useful to get people to just free associate to the belief that they have, or to visualise what that belief means to them. As time has gone by, I have become less concerned with having a perfect sequence and more concerned with getting more information about the various mean-ings associated with the original statement. Once the whole constellation of meaning has been obtained, the statements can easily be put in order by asking the participant to rate each statement according to the degree of emotion associated with it. The SUD scale (e.g. Wolpe 1997) is useful for this. So once a set of statements has been obtained by any method, they can be put in order by collecting all the statements that evoke the same emotion together. The statements can then be ranked according to degree of emotion they evoke. The whole process can then be validated because each set should have a common theme, with the statements becoming more general and absolute and salient for the person as the intensity of emotion increases.

Alternatively, I find it useful to bear in mind that the theme of vertical arrows is often associated with the emotion. Depression is usually associated with thoughts of worth-lessness: the 'I stink' belief or 'alone'. Fear or anxiety is often associated with beliefs about coming to harm, and anger with 'you stink'. Although anxiety and depression may involve the same beliefs, with depression the events have already come true, but in anxiety they are still in the future. In depression the person thinks 'I *am* worthless', 'I will end up alone' but with anxiety it is still not totally certain: 'I will be worthless *if...* ' I *might* end up alone'. You can use this understanding to ask open-ended questions to guide the vertical arrow process, such as 'So what would you be afraid of?'.

For people who are getting stuck after generating a number of statements it may help to use the Cognitive Triad (Beck *et al.*, 1979) to suggest possible content such as 'what would that mean about you as a person?' 'What would that mean about the world?' 'What would that mean about the future?' And if people seem to be near the end, then it may be useful to suggest the specific beliefs that were listed in Session 1, e.g. 'would that mean you were useless or worthless?' (I stink) or 'would you mean you would end up alone.'

Finally, to prevent people going off track because they swap emotions between one statement and the next, it is important to keep asking the question 'does that statement evoke the same emotion as that (the adjacent one in the vertical arrow)?'

Chapter 8

THERAPY SESSION FOUR

GOALS OF SESSION FOUR

1. To consolidate the work on vertical arrows which was introduced last week; to solve any problems participants are having with applying the vertical arrow procedure to identify negative schemas.
2. For participants to be able to recognise ten common types of negative schemas and to be able to categorise their own beliefs into those ten common categories.

SUMMARY OF SESSION FOUR

- Review of homework from previous session
- Lecture A: Review vertical arrow, advanced vertical arrow
- Exercise: Continue vertical arrow
- Lecture B: Types of belief
- Exercise: Categorising beliefs
- Homework for next week

REVIEW OF HOMEWORK FROM SESSION THREE

1. Check that everyone has at least 14 daily A-B-C situations and the 10 worst events in adult life.

> Review of homework is one of the important parts of the program. As with most homework associated with carrying out therapy, it is important to temper the criticism with positive reinforcement. The aim is get at the substantive meaning of the belief to the person and express it in a way that is testable. It is important that the vertical arrow should lead to a greater refinement of the meaning, usually reflected in more general, more absolute statements, with greater degrees of emotional intensity evident as progress is made through the vertical arrow. It is not necessary, however, that each step in the vertical arrow shows clear progression in generality and emotional intensity than the last, since it is sometimes useful just to explore around a particular statement to come to a better understanding of just what It means for the individual.

2. Check that they all have activating events in column A, emotional Consequences in column C, and automatic thoughts at point B.
3. Review vertical arrows, check for form and progression to key/core beliefs, and correct any errors.

LECTURE A: ADVANCED VERTICAL ARROW

For the first half of this session we are going to continue with unpacking the suitcase. Last time I introduced the vertical arrow method of analysing your thoughts, and many of you have been fairly successful in applying this during the week.

The aim last week was simply to get you started on what is probably the most difficult thing you will have to do in cognitive therapy. This week, and for part of next week, we are going to be working on the same task. The aim is that you will be able to analyse all of your A-B-Cs using the vertical arrow, so that you will get as complete a list as possible of the beliefs and negative attitudes which lead to your emotional difficulties, your depression or anxiety or whatever.

It is not necessary to do it perfectly every time. It is a matter of 'all roads lead to Rome'. As you do your vertical arrows you will probably find that you start getting the same chains of thoughts. However, it is important that you do cover all of the situations that cause emotional upset in your life, so you should be on the lookout for A-B-C events which do not fit patterns you know about.

Let's just review the process for a minute:

1. You take an A-B-C event, and choose one of the emotional consequences associated with it. (If there is more than one emotion leave any others till later. Repeat the vertical arrow with each other emotion after you have gone as far as you can with the first one.)
2. You find the automatic thought or irrational belief associated with that emotion.
3. You look at the sentence of the automatic thought. You look for key words. You ask yourself questions like 'If that was true what would it mean to me? Why would that be upsetting to me? If that did happen why would it be so bad?' Trying in each case to get at the *meaning* of each thought or belief to you.
4. You keep doing that until you can go no further. Sometimes that might be after 3 steps, sometimes after 15 or more steps.

The overhead (OHT 26, Figure 8.1) shows some other techniques that might help with your vertical arrows.

Show and explain OHTs 26, 13, & 14 (Figures 8.1 and 8.2)

EXERCISE: MORE VERTICAL ARROWS

Have participants continue with doing vertical arrows for their various A-B-Cs collected earlier.

LECTURE B: CATEGORISING BELIEFS

We are now moving from identifying your beliefs, or unpacking the suitcase, to organising our understanding of those beliefs, or taking stock of them. It is important that you identify as many negative beliefs as possible, so you will need to continue recording

1. Focus on key words.

2. Imagine the situation you are thinking about, or imagine or remember a situation in which you might have the thought you are working on – even exaggerate the situation or carry it to the logical extreme.

3. Be aware of images associated with each belief.
   * visual – as in seeing your father standing over you
   * auditory – hearing his angry voice
   * kinaesthetic – the sensation of falling

4. Investigate meaning in terms of your life history.

5. Specify
   * both halves of conditional sentences. 'If I had a dirty house my mother would hate me' rather than 'My mother would hate me'.
   * the meanings of pronouns: 'My life would be a disaster', not 'It would be a disaster'.
   * all parts of the sentence, e.g. 'I would be a failure at life' not 'I would be a failure'.
   * the exact people 'My brothers would laugh at me' not 'They would laugh at me'.
   * all probabilities 'It is 95% certain that I would not get the job'.

6. Check that the emotion associated with the belief intensifies as you go down the vertical arrow. The bottom core belief should have a powerful emotional impact.

7. When unable to go further ask yourself the more specific questions: If this was true, what would it mean about...
   * me as a person?
   * the world?
   * my future?

8. Key (core) beliefs, which come at the bottom of the vertical arrows can be recognised by
   * their general nature;
   * the statement is usually in the form of an absolute assertion: 'I am/would be worthless', similar to the list of beliefs I gave in the first session.

Figure 8.1. Advanced techniques in vertical arrow

I Stink	I am worthless, no good, of no value.
You Stink	A person who offends me is no good, a total bastard.
Namby-Pamby	I can't stand it, I can't cope, I'll go crazy.
Monster	I am coming to harm, I am sick.
Doomsday	This event is catastrophic, the future is hopeless.
Fairy-tale	Things should be better; the world should be like x.
Alone	I am rejected, I am alone.
Kitten	I am powerless.
Bomb	I am out of control.
Victim	The world/fate/God/the cosmos is unfair, has done me wrong.

Figure 8.2. Common negative core beliefs or schemas

your A-B-Cs and doing your vertical arrows until you are not getting any new information. In the meantime it may be useful for you to learn how to categorise your beliefs.

Beliefs can be classified on two dimensions: content, and generality/intensity. We will deal with the generality/intensity issue in a few sessions' time, but in the meantime it is useful to consider the content dimension. Each belief you identify through doing A-B-Cs or vertical arrows has some kind of content. The main kinds of content are reflected in the list of beliefs on the OHT.

I stink refers to any belief in which you devalue or put down yourself, no matter whether the circumstances are interpersonal or achievement oriented. It includes thinking about yourself as worthless, no good, or even worthless or bad under certain circumstances.

You stink refers to any belief in which you devalue another person, judge them as bad, or that they are bad under specific circumstances, such as not doing what they *should*.

Namby-pamby refers to a belief that an event or person is unbearable.

Monster refers to any belief in which you exaggerate the possibility of harm to yourself under certain circumstances. Beliefs in this category are usually associated with anxiety and fear.

Doomsday refers to any belief in which you exaggerate the possibility of a negative outcome.

Fairy-tale refers to beliefs that specify how the world, including other people, *should* be, or *should* behave.

Alone refers to any beliefs which are associated with rejection by others and being, or ending up, isolated from other people.

Kitten refers to beliefs in which you minimise your ability to deal with particular events or situations.

Bomb refers to beliefs that you may be out of control, or may become out of control under certain circumstances.

Victim refers to beliefs that the world or the cosmos, fate or God, is treating you badly or unfairly.

It is possible, and even probable, that a belief may include content in different categories. For example the belief 'the world should treat me better' may involve *fairy-tale* because you are saying 'the world should be just and fair'. It may involve *victim* because you are saying 'it's not fair to me', and it may involve *you stink*, because you may be saying that the cosmos is no good. It is also possible that your belief involves a category I have not described. If so, try to identify the general theme of the belief. Maybe you'll discover a new category!

EXERCISE: CATEGORISING BELIEFS

What I want you to do now is to categorise all the beliefs you have found so far. Use the initials of the names of the different kinds of belief, e.g. 'IS' for I stink, 'YS' for you stink, and so on.

> *Coach participants to achieve this to identify the correct category as accurately as possible.*

HOMEWORK FOR SESSION FOUR

1. Continue to do vertical arrows until all A-B-Cs have been done, unless the vertical arrow is a clear repetition of others that have been done.

2. Continue belief classification.

People usually find as they continue with vertical arrows that a small number of patterns emerge. These patterns are important and worth noticing. There is no need to continue to do vertical arrows once it seems clear that no new information will be obtained.

PROBLEMS THAT MAY ARISE IN SESSION FOUR

The main problems encountered in this session are concerned with the two main goals of the session: identifying schemas using the vertical arrow procedure, and categorising the beliefs obtained in the vertical arrow procedure into the ten categories of common negative beliefs. Most of the problems encountered with the vertical arrow procedure were described in the last session. A small number of participants may continue to have difficulties. With such people the best approach seems to be scheduling one or more individual sessions to work through a series of vertical arrows with the person. It is usually possible to teach people the vertical arrow procedure in one or two individual sessions, but if a person continues to have considerable difficulty, then it may be necessary to withdraw the person from the group.

An approach I have found quite useful is to bring a participant who is having difficulties into the clinic for a morning or afternoon, and then spending a little time with them and coaching them every half hour or so, in between other activities.

An important consideration at this point in the group program is how comprehensive we want the participants' sets of negative beliefs to be. In general the aim is to get a fully comprehensive set of beliefs for each participant. Some participants for one reason or another will achieve this aim quite quickly and easily within the two weeks assigned for this purpose. Others will not have completed the task before the group is scheduled to move on to the next step in the program. The dilemma for the therapist is whether to slow the program down, postpone moving on to the next step, or carry on as scheduled. I generally go with the majority: if the majority have not completed their vertical arrows I will schedule one extra session, so that participants have opportunity for two hours more group coaching and one more week to work on vertical arrows for homework. I have never done more than one extra session under these circumstances.

There still may be some participants who have not completed their vertical arrows even with the extra time. However, I do not think this matters since, in the first instance there is the opportunity for them to catch up during the next several weeks. In the second instance, it is not essential to have a comprehensive set of beliefs to work through the program. It will be shown in Chapter 16 that clinically effective results can be obtained working through even quite a limited number of vertical arrows. All that is necessary is for the participant to have identified enough beliefs for them to work through the rest of the program.

The other main difficulty people have in this session is in categorising the beliefs correctly. In coaching people to categorise beliefs, it is useful to refer back to the list given in Figure 8.2 and on OHTs 13 and 14. I try to help by pointing out the abstract qualities of the belief and matching these to the abstract qualities of the beliefs on the list. For example I will ask the participant questions like the following: Who or what is the belief about? Is it about yourself, your car, the way the world should be, about another person, or about the future? Then I will ask them which belief on the list also has those qualities.

Another clue is the emotion that is associated with the belief. 'You stink' is usually associated with anger, and anxiety is usually associated either with 'monster', or with a conditional version of one of the beliefs usually associated with depression, such as 'I stink', or 'Doomsday'.

Chapter 9

THERAPY SESSION FIVE

GOALS OF SESSION FIVE

The goals of this session are mostly concerned with the participants coming to some 'big picture' understanding of how their negative beliefs fit together. To this end they make master lists of the negative beliefs, they make 'cognitive maps' of how the beliefs relate to each other, and they rate their beliefs on the SUD scale in terms of the intensity of emotion associated with them.

SUMMARY OF SESSION FIVE

- Review of homework from previous session
- Lecture A: Making a master list of beliefs
- Exercise: Start the master list of beliefs
- Lecture B: Cognitive maps
- Exercise: Making cognitive maps
- Lecture C: Making SUD ratings
- Exercise: SUD ratings
- Homework for next week

REVIEW OF HOMEWORK FROM SESSION FOUR

1. As for Session 4, check vertical arrows for all remaining A-B-C situations.
2. Check belief classification.

> With each person you can note and comment about the categories in which they seem
> to have the highest number of negative beliefs.

LECTURE A: MAKING A 'MASTER LIST' OF BELIEFS

By now you should have 20–30 A-B-Cs analysed by the vertical arrow method. We are now looking at different ways of organising the information you have got about yourself. Many of you will have noticed that the same, or similar thoughts occur time after time. You will probably find that there is a limited number of negative beliefs that you are using in a wide variety of situations. We have already looked at one way of organising them, by putting them into categories and looking at which categories have the largest number of negative beliefs. We are now going to look at a very simple method of organising your beliefs: by making a list of all the *different* beliefs that you have identified using the A-B-C and vertical arrow methods.

A master list of beliefs can be explained by returning to the suitcase analogy. If you unpacked your suitcase you might find you had large numbers of some items: identical brass figurines or T-shirts, for example.

You will remember that the next step is weighing the items. Clearly there is no point in weighing or identifying each brass figurine, or each T-shirt, so you might make a list on which you wrote '10 brass figurines, 17 T-shirts', rather than listing each one separately. So you can do the same thing with the beliefs you have obtained through the vertical arrow technique.

You can make one list if you like, but a useful thing to do is to organise your beliefs in terms of importance. You will remember that we got some beliefs from the beginning of the vertical arrow, which were fairly superficial and situation specific and some from further down which were general and absolute which we called core beliefs, or schemas. We also talked about conditional beliefs such as 'If I am not perfectly successful I am worthless'. So I suggest you make three lists, one for situation specific beliefs, one for conditional beliefs, and one for core beliefs.

> *People can write these lists in exercise books, on sheets of paper, or on the master list of beliefs form that is in Appendix 7. You can show examples of various master lists of beliefs, either your own, or from Appendix 6 OHTs 27–29.*

This is like dividing up the contents of your suitcase into 'very heavy items', 'heavy items', and the rest. It makes sense to separate them out so that you can spend more time deciding which of the heavy items to throw away, rather than waste effort thinking about a light item which is not going to make much difference to the weight of the suitcase.

EXERCISE: MASTER LIST OF BELIEFS

> *Participants continue with vertical arrows and writing up their master list of beliefs.*

LECTURE B: COGNITIVE MAPS

The third way of organising your beliefs is by making cognitive maps. We have looked at organising according to category systems, and by making a master list. In this method you group your thoughts into clusters according to which key belief they lead to. This is like putting the contents of your suitcase into piles according to which country you got them in.

You will remember that a couple of sessions ago I introduced you to the idea that the automatic thoughts that you get on the surface are connected to other automatic thoughts, and to core beliefs deeper inside your mind. I showed you that one belief can set off another in a chain, like dominos in a domino snake.

We believe that it is the core belief, or the one at the end of the chain, that causes the emotional disturbance. The more the automatic thought is like the key belief, the more it is able to set it off, and the stronger is the negative emotion that you feel.

Say, for example, your key belief is that you are worthless. That means that every time there is a suggestion that you are inadequate in any way, your 'worthlessness detector' will fire, and you will feel depressed.

Elicit examples

So if there is something that you think is very important in determining your worth, say being a 'good' mother, then any time you see yourself as inadequate in that area, you will feel more depressed than if the inadequacy is in an area which is unimportant to you.

Of course there are many A-B-C situations, and many chains of automatic thoughts which can lead to the same core belief. It's like a pinball machine when if you hit one of the bumpers, the whole board lights up, or like a house of cards, it doesn't matter which one is knocked but one little bump will bring the whole thing down.

This pattern is kept going by two things. One is that you have probably never examined those core beliefs to see whether they are true or false, so you continue to believe them, out of habit. The other is that the negative emotion becomes 'conditioned' to the core belief. This is a technical term which psychologists use when an emotion becomes linked to a situation, an event, or a thought. You know that if someone has an accident, then they become frightened of travelling in cars. This sort of thing is going on all the time to some degree. If we have a happy experience with something, then a memory of that thing, or going to the same place, will make us feel the emotion again. Things associated with our childhood, or with a love affair or other important experiences, will produce the same emotional reactions we felt at the time.

What we are going to do for the rest of this program is to help you look more closely at your beliefs, and see how many of them are false. Then we are going to get rid of the negative emotion that has become linked to those situations and thoughts.

But first we are going to look at a way of organising your beliefs in terms of a set of 'cognitive maps'. You will probably have found that at least two vertical arrows led to the same core belief. You may even have found that the vertical arrows turned out to be the same for the bottom four or five beliefs. Here are some simplified examples:

Show OHTs 30–32 and discuss them. Refer back to them in the following discussion.

When this happens you can make cognitive maps like the examples on the OHTs, with the core belief at the centre, and the chains of beliefs leading to it, like the branches of a tree.

The procedure for making cognitive maps is as follows. You have already decided which are your 'core beliefs', the beliefs which occur at the bottom of the vertical arrow. Probably you will have the same core belief at the bottom of several vertical arrows. What you need to do next is to code those vertical arrows in some way: by a number, or a coloured spot, or a code word that could stand for the core belief. You then take a large piece of paper, and orient it so that the long side is at the bottom. You then write the core belief in a box in the middle, at the bottom. Next you write in all the vertical arrows which lead to that core belief on the same piece of paper, all leading down to the core belief.

Where several vertical arrows end up with the same core beliefs near the bottom, you can join these together, but this is not essential.

EXERCISE: MAKING COGNITIVE MAPS

Have participants work on cognitive maps until you think they have grasped the concepts and procedure.

LECTURE C: USE OF SUD RATINGS

The final way of organising your beliefs that we are going to consider is to rate each belief in terms of *subjective units of disturbance* (SUDs). This was originally devised by one of the early behaviour therapists, Joseph Wolpe. It is simply a rating of how bad, or disturbed, a belief makes you feel if you believe it is true.

> *Show OHT or give handout of Appendix 11 or refer to a diagram of a thermometer using a Centigrade/Celsius scale.*

There are various scales we could use for this, but we are going to use a 100-point scale like the Celsius temperature scale. On this scale, **100** would refer to the **greatest extreme** that you could possibly feel, of that emotion. **0** would refer to a **total absence** of that emotion, not the opposite of that emotion, and not to any degree of any other emotion. The levels between 0 and 100 refer to various intensities or degrees of the emotion. Every belief in your vertical arrows should be associated with a particular level of emotion, and this is what I want you to write next on your master list of beliefs. We would expect that core beliefs are associated with high SUD levels, conditional core beliefs with fairly high levels of SUDs, and situation specific beliefs with lower levels of SUDs.

I would like you to go through your master list of beliefs now and rate the SUDs for each belief in the space provided (demonstrate). One way of rating SUDs is to imagine how you would feel if that belief was true, or if you know it to be true …

EXERCISE: SUDs RATINGS

> *Have participants work on SUDs ratings until you think they have grasped the concepts and the procedure.*

HOMEWORK FOR SESSION FIVE

1. Continue with vertical arrows.
2. Classify any new beliefs discovered.
3. Complete master list of beliefs, and add new beliefs to it.
4. Continue with making cognitive maps and doing SUD ratings on each belief.

PROBLEMS THAT MAY ARISE IN SESSION FIVE

The master list of beliefs seems to be quite a difficult concept to grasp. People seem to have difficulty thinking about a list that contains all of their beliefs, and that it is the *list* that is important. They tend to think the 'master' refers to the particular beliefs.

A second thing that people have difficulty with is listing each belief only *once*. People think only those beliefs that are worded exactly the same are the same belief. Fixing this is relatively simple. It is just a matter of going through the participants' initial lists and helping them to understand that some of their beliefs are really parallel statements of the same belief, and eliminating all but one of them.

The other major problem people have is of discriminating between the kinds of belief. I have tried several ways of making this easier, using typologies and terms such as key beliefs, non-core beliefs and superficial beliefs. The typology used in this version of the program of situation-specific beliefs, conditional beliefs, and core beliefs seems to be the best so far. Conditional beliefs can be identified by the implied 'if' in the sentence, as in 'I would be all alone if my partner left me'. That leaves the major discrimination to be between situation-specific and more general core beliefs. There are no absolute guidelines for this task. Some beliefs are clearly related to the specific situation in which they occurred, or are more general: 'I am a bad parent'. Only beliefs which are both general and specific cause difficulty, e.g. 'I'm no good at football'. For these beliefs it is a matter of the individual deciding where the dividing line falls for them, or where it falls within a particular set of related beliefs. If it is a belief they think is important, it should go with the core beliefs, or if it is relatively unimportant it can go with the situation-specific beliefs.

Since the main aim of the exercise is for the participants to get an overview of their beliefs, it is not important to get a definitive result, but this can be difficult for many depressed people who find it difficult to think in anything other than black and white terms.

Chapter 10

THERAPY SESSION SIX

GOALS OF SESSION SIX

There are two main aims of this session, and they are both cognitive. The first aim is that the participants accept the idea that beliefs are not immutable, that predominant cultural beliefs change over the course of human history, and that individuals also change their beliefs over the course of time. The second aim is that participants accept that it is possible to consider their beliefs objectively. The first aim is achieved by having participants generate examples of beliefs that have changed over the course of human history and beliefs that they have changed over the course of their lives. This paves the way for the idea that the beliefs they have identified in the vertical arrow procedure can be changed also.

The second aim is achieved by using the examples of the scientific process and the legal process of a judge and jury to develop the concept of objectivity. The judge and jury is an institution that most people are familiar with which has the avowed aim of determining the facts by looking for evidence. The example of science is not as familiar to most people, but it is introduced in the context of a hunt for the Loch Ness monster. Use of both analogies improves the chances that the participants will accept and apply the concept, though in general I have found that the judge and jury analogy works better.

SUMMARY OF SESSION SIX

- Review of homework from previous session
- Lecture A: Do you believe in Father Christmas: beliefs can be changed
- Exercise: In small groups making lists of beliefs which have changed in human history and in the participants' own lives
- Lecture B: Testing beliefs, the Loch Ness Monster analogy, objective (judge and jury) analysis
- Exercise: Objective analysis
- Lecture C: Standard analysis
- Homework for next week

By now a law of diminishing returns should be operating. A-B-Cs and vertical arrows should be producing little if any new information. The various methods of organising beliefs should allow the therapist and the participant to identify clusters and patterns in the beliefs with a relatively small number of themes. If this has not happened, the participant may be having difficulty doing homework. It may be necessary to arrange individual sessions for participants who are falling behind. If the whole group is falling behind it may be worth while delaying moving on to the material in this session until all have completed the preliminary work.

REVIEW OF HOMEWORK FROM SESSION FIVE

Review participants' vertical arrows, A-B-Cs, master lists of beliefs, their classification and SUD levels, and their cognitive maps. Check to make sure that automatic thoughts, core beliefs, etc. are stated in complete sentences with all pronouns specified, no hidden conditionals, etc. Make sure that the sets of beliefs do not contain descriptions of emotional consequences if these can be avoided.

Now is a good time to collect and to make copies of all cognitive maps and master lists of beliefs for your own records. This gives you a 'cognitive diagnosis' for each person.

LECTURE A: DO YOU BELIEVE IN FATHER CHRISTMAS? BELIEFS CAN BE CHANGED

Today we are going to look at how we get some of our beliefs, and how beliefs are changed. First of all, many beliefs have changed throughout the history of humankind, especially as scientists have found out more about the world of nature, or one culture has come into contact with another, or even some beliefs such as religious beliefs can change because of thinking or philosophising. Beliefs can also change because they are no longer fashionable, like last year's colours.

What are some things which were believed some time in history, but which are not believed in (this year)?

Elicit examples such as the world is flat, the Sun goes round the Earth, and write them on the board.

OK, the majority of people in this culture, in the 1990s, do not believe those things we have written up there. The beliefs of large groups of people change over time, usually because the people get some proof that the old belief is wrong. It is hard to believe that the world is flat if someone has managed to sail right around and come back to the starting point. Of course it often takes a long time for society to accept new beliefs, even when there is considerable evidence. There are still people today who believe the world is flat.

The same process applies with individuals. We have all sorts of strange beliefs as children, such as believing in fairies, or superman, or how babies are made. The most common one in our culture is belief in Father Christmas.

What are some things that you once believed that you don't believe any more?

As before elicit examples and write them on the board.

EXERCISE: BELIEFS THAT HAVE CHANGED

In small groups participants make lists of
1. Beliefs held in historical times that are no longer held.
2. Beliefs held by individuals in childhood or otherwise, which they no longer believe in.
3. The reasons they stopped believing that thing.

LECTURE B

Testing your beliefs: the Loch Ness Monster analogy

Imagine you were a person of unlimited financial resources. Holidaying in Scotland you, of course, stay on the shores of Loch Ness. Walking home one misty night after several drinks of the local whisky, you see what seems to be a creature with long neck and a small head in the lake. Was it the mist, the whisky, your imagination, or did you really see the Loch Ness Monster? Well you of course know your own mind, but you want to prove it to the world. How would you do it?

> *Coach patients coming up with various methods, including asking other people, using their own senses, asking experts, etc.*

Well let's say you engage the best scientists, and obtain the latest technology and you search for the monster. Despite all of that you fail to find any evidence. Do you conclude that there is no monster in Loch Ness? What would a scientist conclude? Is it still possible that there was a monster but you didn't look long enough or hard enough, and didn't have sufficiently sensitive equipment?

> *Encourage participants to state that the scientist would have to conclude 'No monster', even though there might be a possibility that developments in technology might eventually provide evidence for the monster.*

Objective analysis: you be the judge and jury

We can do the same for your beliefs as we did for the Loch Ness monster: use the best means available to test them. You need to look very carefully at each belief as if you were a rational scientist, or a judge and jury in a court case. Try to decide whether a belief is true or false by considering the belief in isolation from what it makes you feel. Is the belief true or false according to the facts? You should not decide whether a belief is true or false based on how it makes you feel. Once you have made your master list of beliefs, I want you to consider each belief and decide whether you would consider the belief to be true or false if you were a scientist, or a judge or jury member in a court case. This is called 'objective analysis' because you are trying to be objective and separate out your feelings from the facts.

EXERCISE: OBJECTIVE ANALYSIS

> *Coach people in doing objective analysis until they are able to take an objective attitude, but do not attempt to reason with them over the truth or falsity of a particular belief.*

LECTURE C: STANDARD ANALYSIS

Before the last exercise I introduced you to the idea that you are putting your beliefs 'on trial'. You are like a judge and jury, trying to decide on the basis of evidence whether your beliefs are 'false', i.e. guilty, or 'true'

In a law court the judge often relies on 'precedent', which is the judgements which have been given in similar cases in the past. We can do the same thing in cognitive therapy. Other people with similar problems hold many of the negative beliefs you have discovered. Therapists have developed standard arguments against many of those negative beliefs. We can use these standard arguments to challenge your beliefs.

The first step, of course, is to find out which beliefs are most important for you. We can use the information we have already. Identify the themes which come up most frequently and most powerfully, and then I will direct you to material which will help you to challenge those beliefs.

> *Identify the most common themes in the participant's negative beliefs and prescribe appropriate reading, e.g. chapters from 'A New Guide to Rational Living' (Ellis & Harper, 1975).*

HOMEWORK FOR SESSION SIX

1. Complete master list of beliefs.
2. Complete objective analysis of beliefs identified to date.

PROBLEMS THAT MAY ARISE IN SESSION SIX

In my experience few people have difficulties with the 'beliefs can be changed' aspect of the session, though some people have difficulty accepting that what is true one day may not be true the next, after new discoveries are made. These people may need a little individual work to accept the concept. People do have difficulty maintaining their objectivity in objective analysis. I simply reorient them to the task by asking such questions as 'What evidence is there for and against the belief… well if a judge and jury were looking at that evidence, what would they conclude?' It does not matter if participants do not refute all their beliefs in this session, but it is nice if they do refute some of them. There is ample opportunity in subsequent sessions for participants to challenge and refute even beliefs that are quite complicated.

Chapter 11

THERAPY SESSION SEVEN

GOALS OF SESSION SEVEN

The main goals of this session are for participants to understand that beliefs can be evaluated according to a number of criteria. The content of the session follows on from the previous session in which it was demonstrated that belief change is a natural process in both human culture and individual human beings. In this session three additional ideas are introduced. It is explained that beliefs can have differing degrees of utility, and that the sets of beliefs people use to organise their behaviour can have variable degrees of consistency with each other, and with the beliefs held by other people. Finally, it is argued that consistency with other beliefs and the beliefs of other people have implications for the truth of the belief. The implication of these ideas is that people can evaluate the beliefs on these dimensions as well as the dimension of objective truth. This ties in with one of the major themes of the program, that people are able, through the process of the program, to identify their troublesome beliefs, evaluate them, and decide which they wish to keep and which they wish to discard.

Thus, the goals of the session are that the participants understand these two additional dimensions, and that they successfully rate the beliefs on their master list of beliefs according to these criteria.

SUMMARY OF SESSION SEVEN

- Review of homework from previous session.
- Lecture A: Utility analysis.
- Exercise: Utility analysis.
- Lecture B: Consistency analysis.
- Exercise: Consistency analysis.
- Homework for session seven.

REVIEW OF HOMEWORK FROM SESSION SIX

Review what master list of beliefs should look like at this stage:

- It should be reasonably comprehensive: about 10–30 beliefs seems to be most effective.
- The beliefs should be thematically distinct: lots of beliefs with similar meanings make for unnecessary effort and are best consolidated.

- The beliefs should be organised into separate lists of situation-specific beliefs, conditional schemas, and absolute schemas.
- Beliefs should be categorised into 'namby-pamby', 'monster', etc.
- Ensure all master lists of beliefs are adequate before proceeding.

> This section is based on checklist analysis, developed by Paul Conrad. This version is substantially modified from Conrad's.

LECTURE A: UTILITY ANALYSIS

One of the important things about beliefs is the purpose they serve. We usually start believing a particular belief because we think it is going to stop us from coming to any harm, or because it is going to help us experience pleasant events. We learn these beliefs in childhood, but often they do not serve the same purpose later in life. We do not check them out to see whether they are still useful for us and so we just keep on using them. This kind of pattern applies for the ten problem beliefs introduced earlier.

'Namby-pamby' is essentially a childish belief. If we couldn't stand something as a child our parents would often solve the problem for us. But as adults, of course this belief doesn't do us any good because there is usually no one else to solve the problem. Some people of course do find partners to replace their parents and may live in dependent relationships all their lives.

'Fairy-tale' is similarly a childish belief. Children have difficulty separating real life and fantasy, and they often believe that their parents, or their wishes, are all-powerful. As adults this belief doesn't do us any good because it stops us from setting our goals and working towards them. We spend all our energy wishing rather than working.

'Monster' is also something that comes from our childhood. Clearly there are some things that are dangerous and it is advisable to be careful. Children get taught certain rules ... 'Don't go out on the road'; 'Don't play with matches'. But that doesn't mean that it is always dangerous to go on the road, or that you shouldn't ever touch matches. We may have been punished for something as a child, or learnt to fear something. All these things don't mean that we should obey the same rules as adults when we are able to analyse the risks in a situation for ourselves, or that the harm will still come to us when there is no one to carry out the punishment.

'Monster' can also be acquired in adulthood. If we experience a particularly traumatic event, some aspects of that event may become falsely associated with danger for us. For instance a person who has a car accident may then avoid driving completely. This sort of thing can happen in agoraphobia and panic disorder: the person experiences their own autonomic arousal while waiting at a supermarket check-out, they think the rapid heart-beat and funny feeling means they are going to pass out, die, or something else embarrassing. They then become scared of the same symptoms and may start avoiding supermarkets. What probably caused the autonomic nervous system arousal in the first instance may have been stress that had nothing at all to do with supermarkets. It's just that the check-out line was a time when the person's attention was not involved elsewhere, so they had the opportunity to experience their own autonomic nervous system arousal.

There is one other set of beliefs I want to mention in detail: the *shoulds*. As children, our parents, and adults in general, try to get us to do various things by *invoking the shoulds*. Often we are not told why we *should* do the thing, or we may be punished for *not* doing the thing. Logically, every should needs a reason: you *should* look both ways before crossing the road *if* you don't want to get hit. We are taught shoulds as children because they make the world simpler for us. As adults we are much more capable of assessing the logical consequences of actions for ourselves. As children we often complied with the shoulds to avoid punishment. As an adult there is not the same possibility of being punished. It is important for people to identify their *shoulds* and decide whether they serve any useful purpose in adult life.

Some of the other common problem beliefs follow the same pattern, but some are never useful. *I stink*, for example, may explain to a child why he or she is being treated so badly, but the associated loss of self-esteem is probably not worth it.

Can any of you see how some of the other common negative schemas are not useful, even though they may once have been?

Spend some time eliciting discussion as to how the other common negative schemas are not particularly useful in adulthood even if they were adaptive in childhood.

Today we are going to look at whether the beliefs on your master list of beliefs serve any useful purpose for you. We can do this by asking three questions:

1. Does the belief make me feel any better?
2. Does the belief help me to accomplish my goals?
3. Does the belief help me get along better with others?

For any particular belief, the more of these questions you answer 'no' to, the less likely it is that the belief is serving you any useful purpose. If, for example, you answer no to all three questions, then you are saying that:

1. The belief is not making you feel any better. It may even be making you feel worse.
2. The belief is not helping you achieve your goals … in fact, it may be actively preventing you from accomplishing your goals.
3. The belief is not helping you get on better with others. It may even be harming your relationships with others.

So you can see that if you answer 'no' to those questions, then the belief is not doing you any good. In fact it is very likely that the belief itself is causing you to suffer, or making you less efficient in achieving your goals, managing your life, getting on with people, etc.

Of course finding out that a belief is causing you harm, or is preventing you from achieving your goals, or serves no useful purpose for you, doesn't mean that it's automatically false. Asking those questions may help you to decide that the belief is false. Even if you can't conclude that it *is* false, you may well be able to conclude that you would be better off without that particular belief.

EXERCISE: UTILITY ANALYSIS

You will notice that the Master List of Beliefs form has boxes for all the questions and a space beside to decide whether the belief is useful, (UF); or useless, (UL). For each belief on your master list of beliefs you need to answer the three questions and then decide whether the belief is useful or useless.

Demonstrate, and then have participants do utility analysis on all beliefs on their master lists of beliefs.

LECTURE B: CONSISTENCY ANALYSIS

Another way of deciding whether a belief is true or not is to find out how consistently it is believed. If a person tends to have a belief in some situations, but to believe something quite different in other similar situations, then the indications are that the belief is false, or at least suspect. If a person believes at times when his or her heart 'misses a beat' that they are going to have a heart attack and die, and on other occasions disregards the sensation, then the belief requires further consideration, which might lead to it being declared 'false'. Belief is not necessarily a black or white phenomenon. We have varying degrees of uncertainty about many of our beliefs. Agnosticism is somewhere between belief in God and atheism, for example. Any uncertainty in a belief, such as only believing at some times that you are really worthless, may indicate that you are thinking more rationally at other times, and may indicate that the belief is 'false' on *all* occasions. You can't really be worthless only part of the time.

Consistency analysis is done in three steps on the master list of beliefs. First answer yes or no to the question 'Do I always think this way, believe this, in similar situations?' Second, you ask yourself 'would others always have this belief in similar circumstances?' Of course people in this world have vastly different beliefs. There are still people who believe the world is flat. But unless you have special knowledge, if your belief is different from what most people of your background and culture would think in similar circumstances, then there is a high probability that your belief is false.

Finally you decide whether those answers mean your belief is true or false and you write your answer in the box.

Demonstrate on OHP or blackboard.

EXERCISE: CONSISTENCY ANALYSIS

Have participants complete the consistency analysis section of the master list of beliefs.

HOMEWORK FOR SESSION SEVEN

Complete utility analysis and consistency analysis for all beliefs on the master list of beliefs.

PROBLEMS THAT MAY ARISE IN SESSION SEVEN

There are few difficulties with the session. The main therapist action that is required is to help the participants to understand what is required and to ensure that they follow the steps correctly. To assist participants in determining utility it is often necessary to ask questions such as 'In what way does that belief affect your behaviour?' 'Does that have good or bad outcomes for you?', and 'Does that make the belief useful or useless?' To assist participants in determining consistency you may also need to focus their thinking by thinking of situations in which they wouldn't think that way and asking them about those situations. For example: 'When someone comments about your child and says how well behaved she is, do you think you're a lousy parent at that time?' When there are inconsistencies you can draw their attention to them 'so if you think that sometimes you're a lousy parent and other times that you're an OK parent, is it possible to be both? Which is true then? So does that make the belief that you're a lousy parent false?'

Chapter 12

THERAPY SESSION EIGHT

GOALS OF SESSION EIGHT

The goal of this session is that participants are able to apply the logical analysis procedure to their beliefs. The logical analysis procedure is the most powerful technique for challenging people's beliefs, but it is also conceptually the most difficult. The process is very similar to that involved in experiments in the social sciences, so most therapists will be familiar with it. To carry out the process participants need to understand the individual steps of *stating your case, defining your terms, deciding your rules, finding and examining your evidence, and stating your verdict.*

Stating your case is like refining your experimental question. It is important to identify exactly what the person's belief actually is. Sometimes it is more important to identify the underlying principle such as 'A person is worthless if they are not successful in their occupation', and sometimes it is more important to specify the belief with reference to the individual: 'I am not successful'. Sometimes it can be useful to do both. An important aspect of logical analysis is that there are multiple ways of challenging the belief. One of the tasks of the therapist is to guide the participant into doing a logical analysis that works for them. This means the therapist has to aim the analysis at a conceptual level that is likely to be understood by the participant. Since part of logical analysis involves appealing to other superordinate beliefs and values, then it helps to orient the logical analysis to be consistent with these superordinate beliefs and values. It is not a good idea to define a belief for testing in terms that involve the participant's most deep-seated prejudices. If you wish to examine these prejudices then that is better done separately.

Defining your terms is similar to the process of operational definition in social science research. It is a matter of defining the belief in terms of phenomena that (a) are observable, and (b) are an acceptable expression of the principle that is at issue. It is important to avoid very idiosyncratic definitions of concepts such as 'failure'. There are multiple ways in which any belief can be operationally defined, but the following principles are useful. The definition should be:

- acceptable to the participant;
- consistent with beliefs in the participant's subculture;
- testable with reasonable ease.

Deciding your rules is like setting up the parameters of the experiment: sample size, planned comparisons, type I error rate, and so on. Setting in advance the procedure of the experiment and the evidence that you would accept as disconfirming your hypothesis or supporting your hypothesis is an important principle of research.

To some degree logical analysis is concerned with attempting to disconfirm the negative beliefs. The main job of the therapist in this session is to encourage the participant to develop the logical analysis that is most effective at disconfirming the particular belief. To some extent this involves being familiar with the subculture the participant comes from and his or her likely basic beliefs and values. This understanding is then used to create a tension between the participant's basic beliefs and values and the negative belief being analysed such that the participant can conclude that the negative belief is false.

SUMMARY OF SESSION EIGHT

- Review of homework from previous session
- Lecture A: Logical analysis
- Exercise: Logical analysis
- Homework for next week

The main topic for this session is logical analysis, which is one of the more difficult skills in cognitive therapy. It was developed by McMullin and Giles (1981), and further explicated by McMullin (1986). My version is somewhat modified. Examples of logical analysis using a special form are contained in Appendix 8, as well as a blank copy of the form in Appendix 9. The examples are referred to in the lecture, and are useful to assist participants in learning the process. The forms can be photocopied and handed out or they can be put onto OHTs. To show the whole form the writing has to be fairly small, so I suggest that even if you do use OHTs it is desirable that participants have a printed copy to refer to and to take home.

REVIEW OF HOMEWORK FROM SESSION SEVEN

Check that utility analysis and consistency analysis have been done for all beliefs.

LECTURE A: LOGICAL ANALYSIS

You will probably remember the Loch Ness Monster story that we used in the last session. In this analogy we came up with a number of ways of deciding whether there really was a monster in Loch Ness. This next technique is a way of defining and analysing our beliefs very carefully, like planning a detailed program of research to provide the most definitive evidence possible at the time about whether there is a monster in Loch Ness. One of the most powerful ways of checking out our beliefs is to analyse our beliefs very carefully and then to test them. This is called logical analysis, and it may include setting up experiments to see whether the beliefs are true or false. The process of doing logical analysis is much the same as a scientist uses in setting up an experiment.

In order to determine whether a belief or statement is true, we must have three things:

1. knowledge of the statement's meaning;
2. knowledge of the right way to test it;
3. good evidence for believing it.

When we actually analyse beliefs, this can be converted into a five-step process:

1. State your case.
2. Define your terms.
3. Decide your rules.
4. Find and examine your evidence.
5. State your verdict.

Let's look at them one at a time.

Stating your case

Use the Loch Ness monster example or another, using the logical analysis worksheet.

You first have to state your thoughts meaningfully.
   Here are some suggestions for doing this:

- *Specify both halves of conditional sentences.* 'If I had a dirty house my mother would hate me' rather than 'My mother would hate me'.
- *Specify the meanings of pronouns*: 'My life would be a disaster', not 'It would be a disaster'.
- *Specify all parts of the sentence:* 'I would be a failure at life' not 'I would be a failure'.
- *Specify the exact people:* 'My brothers would laugh at me' not 'They would laugh at me'.
- *Specify all probabilities:* 'It is 95% certain that I would not get the job'.

I have been trying to help you do this as we've gone through the vertical arrows and making up the master list of beliefs by asking you to leave out descriptions of emotional consequences and to be as specific as possible.
   Another approach is to identify the *principle* that underlies your statement, so rather than 'I will be worthless if I am not successful at my profession', 'A person who is unsuccessful in their profession is therefore worthless.' Sometimes it is useful to consider a belief as it relates to you, sometimes in terms of the general principle, sometimes as both.

Defining your terms

The same word may mean different things to different people, and sometimes people have the wrong idea about what a word means. The most common one I come across is 'nervous breakdown'. People have vastly different ideas of what a 'nervous breakdown' is, and I'm not sure whether anyone really knows what it means. I certainly don't. So, when a person has the belief 'I will have a nervous breakdown if things go wrong again', we have to understand what that person means by a nervous breakdown.
   To achieve the best result we have to define all the major terms in our sets of beliefs and we have to define them as concretely and specifically as we can. For example, we might say 'people will hate me if ...' when the main thing we are concerned about is 'my mother will hate me'. 'Mother' is more specific than 'people'. Or a person might believe 'I will lose control of myself and hurt my children', which is more specific and more concrete than 'I will have a nervous breakdown.' The important thing about defining your terms is to come to a publicly acceptable meaning for the words. A dictionary definition can be useful, or you can ask other people. The main thing is to find out whether the facts fit the meaning of the words. Here is an example:

Show 'catastrophe' example, pointing out how 'catastrophe' was defined.

You can see in this example how the person used the word 'catastrophe', and probably thought in terms of the meaning of the word, but it can be seen that the facts are not consistent with the publicly accepted meaning of 'catastrophe'.

It is also important to be specific and concrete, and not to be vague about the meaning of any word.

Show OHT of 'alone' example, pointing out how 'alone' was defined.

In this example you can see how it was important to be very specific about what 'alone' meant to this person.

Just as it is important to specify the terms as concretely as possible it is also necessary to specify levels of probability. An example of specifying probability is this logical analysis:

Show 'appeasement' OHT. Point out how crucial the specification of the probability of harm was in the analysis.

You can see from the example that specifying the probability makes it possible to test the truth or falsity of this belief.

Deciding your rules

Before you go out and look for evidence, it is important that you decide what facts you would need to prove your belief true and what facts you would need to prove it false. For many beliefs there is not any final answer, because the belief is about the future, or about a chance event. You have to state what you believe is an acceptable risk as best you can. If you were going to decide you didn't have cancer, how many doctors would you consult before you were prepared to accept the risk? The same sort of thing can be done even with the belief 'I'm going to have a nervous breakdown'.

In every case it is important to identify the general relationship or principle implicit or explicit in the belief, and then think of ways to disprove that principle or general relationship. In the Loch Ness monster example the general principle is 'there is a monster in Loch Ness', not 'I saw a monster in Loch Ness'.

It is also important to decide what method you are going to use to get your information, and how much information you are going to try to get. It is important that you decide what amount of information you would accept, and then accept when you have gone through the process, or you will be like the person with cancer who keeps going to one more doctor to get the diagnosis changed. This is like the Loch Ness monster example in that the billionaire had to decide when he was going to accept the verdict of the best technology he could buy. Scientists know that they can only test their hypotheses with the technology and knowledge available to them at the time. As technology and knowledge develop new discoveries will be made, new theories developed and new truth discovered. Hence the continued and repeated efforts to look for a monster in Loch Ness.

There are five main ways of getting evidence.

1. using your senses, either by observation, or by devising an experiment;
2. asking an authority;
3. finding out what most people think;
4. using reason and logic, i.e. 'thought experiments';
5. using your own experience, i.e. your own memories.

You have to choose the most appropriate and efficient method for each belief. You can use the formula: 'True if... and False if...' such as 'True if all five of my teachers say I'm failing, False if even one of my teachers says my work is satisfactory.'

Once you have defined the meaning of your statement there are many ways in which you can test the truth of the statement. Here are some examples of different approaches:

Go through 'who's who' and 'worthless' pointing out the different approaches.

Examining the evidence

This may involve effort: writing to or phoning experts, reading books, conducting experiments, trying out some new behaviour, such as being deliberately rude to see if people reject you, or it may involve using your own reasoning and powers of logic.

Deciding your verdict

This of course follows from all the other steps, and it should be easy if you have done the other steps well. You simply write the result on your logical analysis worksheet, and write the result in the appropriate column on your master list of beliefs.

DEMONSTRATION AND EXERCISE: LOGICAL ANALYSIS

Take some examples and work through them, then have participants start doing logical analyses of their own.

LECTURE B: LOGICAL ANALYSIS CONTINUED

You've now had the chance to do at least one logical analysis, and perhaps you can see how powerful they are. But even if you were not able to decide that your belief was false, that's not the end of it. There is always more than one way of doing logical analysis for a particular belief, and you only have to find that a belief is false once. So, if you have not been able to challenge a belief successfully you can keep on trying.

If someone was to say that someone you loved was a totally bad and evil person, you would keep trying to counter his or her arguments, and you would try all sorts of arguments, wouldn't you? Or if someone tried to say that something important to you was a load of nonsense, you'd do the same, you'd use lots of arguments. The same thing applies with logical analysis: you can keep on trying new ways of testing the belief.

Moreover, it's not necessary to prove that there is no truth at all in a negative belief. Because the beliefs which cause emotional distress are usually absolute, or black and white statements like 'I'm no good', all you have to do is find one small piece of evidence against them for them to be false. A similar, relative belief, such as 'I'm relatively mediocre at x' is less likely to cause emotional problems than 'I am no good'.

We are now going to spend the rest of the session doing logical analysis.

EXERCISE: LOGICAL ANALYSIS

Participants do further logical analysis on their beliefs.

HOMEWORK FOR SESSION EIGHT

Complete logical analysis, especially on beliefs that are still true, and all conditional and absolute schemas.

PROBLEMS THAT MAY ARISE IN SESSION EIGHT

The main problems encountered in this session include participants having difficulty with relative truth, participants defining their beliefs 'reasonably', and participants failing to follow a consistently logical theme throughout the analysis. The most common problem is participants getting 'stuck' either in rewriting their belief as a testable statement, or in deciding upon a method.

Some people have difficulties accepting that one can define 'truth' as being the results of a specified investigation. Sometimes it is necessary to remind them about the progress of science, and that truth is always just the truth at this moment in time with the resources we have to investigate the universe.

By this time many participants will have figured out that it is the absolute nature of their negative beliefs that makes them false. They may try to define their beliefs in quite reasonable terms such as 'I might not survive if my partner left me', which then becomes 'I would find it emotionally and financially difficult if my partner left me', which becomes 'My income would be reduced if my partner left me'. It is useful to ask the participant if they would feel as bad if that was the belief they had and encourage them to redefine the belief in terms that would cause them to feel as bad as they originally did when they had the belief. Or it may help to ask them what was the belief they had when they originally did the A-B-C and vertical arrow.

It is important that each logical analysis follows a logical theme. One of the common problems is that the participant goes 'off track' and defines the belief in terms that only peripherally reflect the critical parts of the original belief. One of the important things to do during coaching is to check that each step reflects the most important parts of the original belief. Participants can usually be guided by asking questions about what they see as the most important part of the original belief, the key words, and then asking whether each successive stage gets at the critical issues.

The same approach can be used if the person gets 'stuck': ask them what is the key issue in the original belief, what are the important words, what do those words mean to them. To help with definitions it is sometimes useful to use a dictionary, or to discuss the word with other group members. To help with finding and examining the evidence it may help to focus the participant by asking them to generate how they might investigate the belief by each method in turn, and then choosing the one they think is most powerful. In fact, at all times in logical analysis it is important to try to make the analysis as powerful as possible.

Chapter 13

THERAPY SESSION NINE

GOALS OF SESSION NINE

There are two main goals of this session: for the participants to be able to construct hierarchies of situations associated with core beliefs, and for the participants to be able to generate counters to their negative beliefs. The hierarchies are similar to the hierarchies used in traditional systematic desensitisation (e.g. Wolpe, 1997), and guidelines used in systematic desensitisation can be followed in the construction of these hierarchies.

As things have been arranged in this program, participants should by now have identified clusters of beliefs centred on one or more core beliefs. These will have been developed during the cognitive mapping section of Session 5. The aim of this session is that the participants complete a hierarchy for each cluster of beliefs before next session. With respect to countering, the aim for this session is that participants start the process, which can then be continued over the next few sessions. It is sufficient in this session that the participant understands the idea of counters and is at least able to develop one or two within the session.

SUMMARY OF SESSION NINE

- Review of homework from previous session
- Lecture A: Hierarchy construction
- Exercise: Generate at least one hierarchy
- Lecture B: Countering
- Exercise: Start to develop counters
- Homework for next week

The procedures in the remaining three sessions require (a) that all important negative beliefs have been declared false, and (b) that the participant has a clear idea of what their negative thinking entails, and how it fits together. For these reasons, it may be necessary to spend an extra session on logical analysis, or to arrange separate sessions for people who have not yet decided cognitively that *all* their beliefs are false. It is also important to ensure that participants have organised their beliefs adequately, particularly that they have completed their cognitive maps.

REVIEW OF HOMEWORK FROM SESSION EIGHT

1. Check numbers of beliefs still considered true.
2. Check logical analyses.
3. Check belief organisation.

LECTURE A: HIERARCHY CONSTRUCTION

Today is exciting, because today we start actively trying to change your beliefs. Many of you will have noticed that your beliefs have changed already, when you have analysed them with objective analysis, or when you have used standard analysis, utility analysis, or logical analysis. This seems to be a somewhat automatic process, a bit like Archimedes and his Eureka experience when he figured out how to determine whether the crown was gold. This seems to be one way of changing beliefs: by acquiring new and contrary information. Another way is by actively trying to think differently, like trying to change a swimming stroke, or a golf swing. Just like any of those skills, at first it is hard to change, but eventually the new behaviour replaces the old. This is what we will be trying in the second section of the session.

> Voluntary cortical inhibition is a kind of combination of imaginal systematic desensitisation and thought stopping developed by McMullin and Giles (1981) and McMullin (1986). I construe it within a Wolpeian model, i.e. that it allows for deconditioning of the emotion attached to various stimuli and thoughts, by means of reciprocal inhibition, as well as allowing for imaginal rehearsal of the new beliefs.

Some of you may have noticed that even though you have changed the belief it still makes you feel bad, whether that is angry, sad or anxious. Has anyone noticed that? Well that's partly because the emotion is still connected to the belief, and to situations that evoke that belief. In these cases we may have to weaken that connection, and we do that by a special procedure called voluntary cortical inhibition (VCI).

Imagine you were going to teach a child who is afraid of water to swim. You would probably try to reduce the child's fear of water, by getting the child used to water in slow stages. You would start by getting the child to dangle his or her feet in the water, get the child into the water up to the child's knee level, up to waist level, and work up to getting the child to put his or her head under. In this way we reduce the negative emotion of fear of water, and this is how VCI works.

In the first half of the session today we are going to make some preparations for doing VCI, and that will be based on the cognitive maps that you did a few weeks ago.

You will remember that in the third session I explained that automatic thoughts occur at the surface of our awareness, and that these automatic thoughts are related to core beliefs or schemas that are well below the surface. It is the core beliefs that are associated with negative emotions, so that every time the core belief is stimulated, or 'hooked', we feel the negative emotion. The closer the automatic thought is to the core belief, the stronger we will feel that negative emotion. In the vertical arrows we did we traced those links, and discovered the core beliefs that really drive our emotion, and later we represented this information in cognitive maps.

The first step in VCI is the construction of a *hierarchy* of situations for each of your core beliefs.

You may have noticed that even though the same core belief is involved in some

> You will note that this is a fairly standard Wolpeian explanation for the decondi-
> tioning of emotion.

situations but not in others, you do not get the same intensity of emotion for all situations involving the same core belief. Who has noticed that?

Well, we capitalise on that by making a list, or hierarchy, of situations that evoke that
particular core belief, and by then desensitising you to those situations, starting with the
less disturbing ones, while you are relaxed. The relaxation acts to inhibit the emotion you
feel when you visualise those situations and think the negative thoughts.

Before we start making hierarchies, we have to review the concept of subjective units
of disturbance (SUDs).

Distribute copies of the Negative Emotion Scale (Appendix 11).

The SUDs scale is like the Celsius or Centigrade temperature scale. There are one
hundred degrees on the scale. 0 degrees (freezing point) is the total absence of that
emotion. 100 degrees (boiling point) is as much of that emotion as you can possibly
imagine. Of course there are various degrees of emotion in between, and that is why
SUDs are so important.

EXERCISE: HIERARCHY CONSTRUCTION

Now what I want you to do is to start a hierarchy for one of your core beliefs. Then think
of a situation which would give you 100 SUDs for that belief, and one which would give
you a low level of SUDs, say about 0–10, but which still evokes that belief. Then think of
a situation that is about halfway between the two in intensity of emotion, say about
50–60 SUDs. Then fill in the gaps until you get 10–15 items 10–15 SUDs apart. You may
find it helpful to look at your original A-B-C situations.

*Help participants to create hierarchies just as for systematic desensitisation. There
are examples in OHTs 33 and 34.*

LECTURE B

Countering

In the last sessions we have been analysing your trouble-making thoughts, and you have
seen that many of them, if not all of them, are false or irrational. Today you are going to
learn how to get rid of those thoughts, to 'take them to the dump'. For many people this
is not easy. Most people cannot say to themselves 'that belief is false' and never think it
again. Let's just for a moment suppose that you wanted to change someone else's mind,
i.e. change their beliefs. How would you do it?

Encourage participants to come up with some of the following methods:

- provide them with some new information;
- argue with them;
- threaten them;
- find some inconsistency, either in their logic, or with other beliefs they hold;
- tell them that people they admire think the way you want them to think;
- repeat the alternative belief many times in their presence.

Well, countering is all of those things, but you do it to your self. To do countering you need counters: beliefs that will inhibit your original negative beliefs, and that will eventually replace them.

The following is the definition of a counter:

Put up overhead with definition of a counter on it; see Appendix 6, OHT 35.

A counter is . . . a thought which argues against another thought and includes such activities as thinking or behaving in the opposite direction, arguing in a very assertive fashion, and convincing oneself of the falsity of a belief.

Characteristics of counters

> The first six of these characteristics or rules are as specified by McMullin & Giles (1981). (Reproduced by permission of Grune & Stratton, Inc.)

And these are the characteristics of counters:

Put up OHT 36.

1. **Counters must be directly opposite to the false belief.** For example, if the false belief were 'I'm worthless if I fail this test', a directly opposite counter would be 'My mark in this test has nothing to do with my worth as a person.'
2. **A counter must be a believable statement of reality**. For example, 'I don't need everyone to love me to be happy' is a reasonable statement. 'It doesn't matter at all if no one likes me' is not.
3. **The client should develop as many counters as possible**. The more counters the better. Develop as many counters as possible for each core belief (and associated surface beliefs).
4. **The counters must be the client's, not the therapist's.** The counters need to be phrased in the client's everyday language to be effective.
5. **Counters must be concise.** Counters are usually more effective if they are short and intense, though there are exceptions. Sometimes **counters may be philosophical.** Philosophical counters discuss the client's basic philosophy about life, and may be quite long. In philosophical counters the client argues with a negative philosophy of life by building an argument which contradicts a negative philosophy of life in a series of steps. For example a person might argue against a philosophy that winning is everything, and that only the toughest and most self-interested survive, by developing a philosophy of humanitarian concern for people who are seen as less fortunate.
6. **Counters must be stated with assertive, aggressive and/or emotional intensity.**
7. **Counters should be as strong as possible.** A strong counter is one that argues directly with the strongest core belief in the chain. For example if the core belief is 'I am worthless', and above it in the vertical arrow is 'I am a bad parent and therefore I am worthless'. In this case, 'I am worthwhile simply because I exist' is a strong counter, and 'I am worthwhile because I am a good parent' is a weaker counter.

Unmodified negative thinking

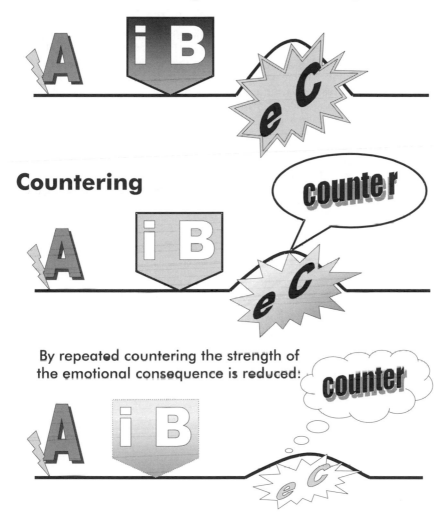

Countering

By repeated countering the strength of
the emotional consequence is reduced:

Eventually the irrational belief is replaced by
a rational belief (rB) and no emotional consequence occurs

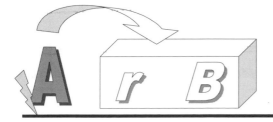

Figure 13.1. The process of countering

How countering works

Put up OHT 37 and explain the diagram in the following terms. See also Figure 13.1.

The diagram shows the effects of countering on the emotional consequence and the development of alternate rational beliefs. The top panel shows the situation when an activating event occurs at point A followed by an unmodified irrational belief. The thin black line shows your emotional level, with the hump being your reaction to the irrational belief. The next panel shows the result of countering: it reduces the emotional reactions. Eventually (bottom panel) the irrational belief is replaced by a rational belief, which may be the counter or developed from the counter, and there is no emotional reaction. So countering works just like learning a new skill, like learning to rollerblade. Even more accurately, countering is like learning a more correct way to perform a skill, like correcting a golf swing or a swimming stroke. At first you have to concentrate to change your way of doing things, then after practice it becomes automatic.

So the next thing to do is to develop counters for all your beliefs, and start using them. To get you started we can try to develop counters for the list of common negative beliefs (OHTs 13 & 14).

EXERCISE: COUNTERING

Show OHTs 13 & 14. Have the participants divide a piece of lined paper into two columns, put the negative beliefs in one column and then write counters in the other.

HOMEWORK FOR SESSION NINE

Show OHT 38. Demonstrate how to write negative beliefs and counters on index cards as on Figure 13.2.

1. Develop counters for all beliefs on master list.
2. Develop evidence for your counters.
3. Complete hierarchies for all core beliefs and transfer to index cards, one scheme per card, including negative thoughts and counters.

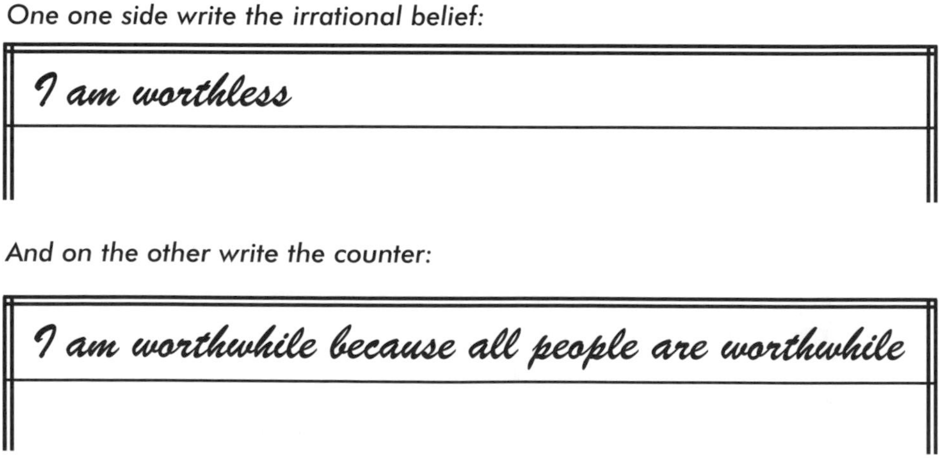

One one side write the irrational belief:

I am worthless

And on the other write the counter:

I am worthwhile because all people are worthwhile

Figure 13.2. Countering using index cards

The counters can be done in two columns as for the exercise, or they can be done on 10 × 15 cm index cards as shown on the OHT.

PROBLEMS THAT MAY ARISE IN SESSION NINE

The problems encountered with hierarchy construction are similar to those encountered in hierarchy construction for systematic desensitisation: too much space between hierarchy items, too few items, and deviation from the main theme or dimension of the hierarchy. To prevent deviation from the main theme, the therapist should scrutinise every hierarchy and coach the participants so that each item represents just a little more saliency to the individual, and just a more intense version of the situation before it and so on up the hierarchy. This may mean just drawing to the participant's attention some departures from the main theme, or it may involve suggesting further items.

The same principle can be followed to address the problem of too few hierarchy items, or too big a gap between items. The therapist can look at the other items in the hierarchy and ask questions like 'What would be a situation in which you would have that belief when the outcome would be more important to you?' or 'What is a situation which would come between that one and that one in intensity of emotion and which has the same characteristics?'

The main difficulties people have with counters include generating them in the first place, and generating counters which are not consistent with the rules of countering. Some deviation from the rules is acceptable, but any one counter should be consistent with most of the rules. Moreover, the same rule should not be broken consistently throughout the set of counters.

Assisting participants to generate counters is a bit more difficult, since the counters need to be stated in the participant's everyday language. It helps to understand the participant's subculture, and basic value structure. The therapist can try initially to coach the participant by using the rules of countering as prompts, such as 'what is a statement which is definitely opposite to that belief?' 'How can that counter be made stronger, or more directly opposite to your negative belief?' The knowledge of the participant's vernacular, subculture, and basic value structure can be used to suggest counters, although it is important to make clear that they are examples only. It is also a good idea to give the participant a number of sample counters to choose from rather than just one.

Chapter 14

THERAPY SESSION TEN

GOALS OF SESSION TEN

There are two main content areas in Session Ten: perceptual shift and voluntary cortical inhibition. The goals for the perceptual shift section are:

- That the participants understand that a set of information can be seen in multiple ways as demonstrated by the ambiguous figures.
- That the participants understand that perceptual shifting is partly an act of will, partly looking at the detail of the information.
- That the participants learn to generate components for perceptual shifting: the counters, the broad category of evidence supporting the counter and some items of detailed evidence supporting the counter.

The goals for the voluntary cortical inhibition section are:

- That the participants understand the procedure for voluntary cortical inhibition sufficiently to do it at home and have experienced it at least briefly.

SUMMARY OF SESSION TEN

- Review of homework from previous session
- Lecture A: Perceptual shift
- Exercise: Filling out perceptual shift forms
- Lecture B: Voluntary cortical inhibition
- Exercise: Voluntary cortical inhibition in large group
- Homework for next week

REVIEW OF HOMEWORK FROM SESSION NINE

Check hierarchies for:

- adherence to core theme;
- correct spacing.

Check counters for

- oppositeness;

- directness;
- strength;
- conciseness;
- intensity.

> The important criteria for counters are that they are (a) potent, and (b) meaningful for the person, so some compromises can be made concerning the above features.

LECTURE A: PERCEPTUAL SHIFT

As you will recall, we have unpacked your suitcase of beliefs, we have weighed them up and found them wanting, and now we are working on getting those emotions to the dump. Last week and for homework you did basic countering, in which you begin to argue with yourself using statements which go against, or contradict, your negative beliefs. This is the simplest and possibly the best technique.

The next way of changing your beliefs is called perceptual shift. It is a special kind of countering, and is especially useful in times of crisis. Like many of the techniques in this program, it was developed by Rian McMullin (McMullin & Giles, 1981; McMullin, 1986).

As I have said in the past, we perceive meaning from the events around us. Sometimes that meaning is mistaken, or sometimes there are other ways we can perceive a particular event.

This is a bunch of black lines, but what do you perceive it as? It is also possible to perceive it as an old or young woman, some people see one, and some see the other. The trick is to be able to see both interpretations of the picture and then to switch from one to the other by act of will. This is done by focusing on the details.

Figure 14.1. Old/young woman (by W.E. Hill; originally published in *Puck*, 1915; later reproduced by Boring (1930) and McMullin (1986))

McMullin (1986, p. 95) provides the following list of details that relate to each picture.

Old Woman	Young Woman
Tip of nose	Tip of chin
Eye	Ear
Mouth	Neckband
Wart on nose	Nose
Looking at us	Looking away
Chin	Lower neck
Hair on nose	Eyelash

Coach participants to see both pictures to do this, and help them to change from one to the other. If necessary, help them to change by shifting their focus onto different details of the picture.

This is similar to how we change *beliefs* in perceptual shift. We concentrate on details of the evidence for the counter(s) and against the negative belief, which directs our attention to the new way of thinking. We also direct our attention even further away from the negative aspects of a situation than we would with basic countering.

There are two main ways of doing perceptual shift. One is to expand the index card approach we used for countering. On the back of the card write the evidence for the counter, as shown on the OHT.

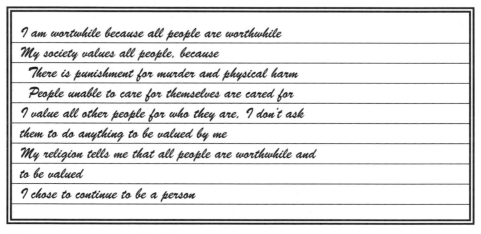

Figure 14.2. Perceptual shift, using cards

Show OHT of Perceptual Shift using cards: OHT40, Figure 14.1.

Or you can do it with just a piece of paper. There are seven steps:

1. You take a piece of paper and divide it into four columns, or you can use a perceptual shift worksheet (Appendix 10). The advantage of a piece of paper is you can take as much vertical space as you need for each negative thought. It is probably good to use the piece of paper sideways or as 'landscape' rather than 'portrait' configuration.
2. At the top of the page you write the situation, such as 'I overheard a friend criticising me', and the emotion, such as 'sad and depressed'.
3. You then write the beliefs or automatic thoughts associated with that situation down the left-hand column.
4. In the next column you write 'true' or 'false'. You may have this information from your

master beliefs list, but if not you may need to go through one of the procedures which you used to falsify your other beliefs: objective analysis, checklist analysis, or logical analysis.

5. In the next column you list a general counter for each of the beliefs or negative automatic thoughts. This might be something like 'A person can be happy even if people dislike him or her.'

6. You then come up with reasons, images, memories, logical arguments, experiences, knowledge, or experiments that make up evidence that the general counter is true. Some examples are 'Lots of public figures are happy despite being disliked by thousands of people'; 'I have got over a person not liking me many times in the past.' You put these detailed counters in the *evidence* column.

7. You then think about the first belief on the list and concentrate on memorising it and each detailed counter until all have come clearly to mind for a minute or longer, and repeat this process with every troublesome belief for that situation.

EXERCISE: PERCEPTUAL SHIFT

Do perceptual shift for a cluster of beliefs associated with one core belief, i.e. one cognitive map.

Perceptual shift was also developed by McMullin and Giles (1981). A number of adaptations of the technique are presented in McMullin (1986).

LECTURE B

Review

Before proceeding, check the following points with the participants.

1. Do you agree that your problems are mainly caused by your beliefs?
2. Do you think we have identified the beliefs that are causing the problem? Have we missed any?
3. Do you know what your core beliefs are?
4. Are all the important ones false?
5. Do you know how to analyse your beliefs so that you can determine whether they are true or false?

Address any doubts or problems before proceeding. It is also a good idea to make sure participants have at least one hierarchy with the lowest five items complete before proceeding with voluntary cortical inhibition.

VCI preparation

So now you know that some of your troublemaking thoughts, or even all of them, are false. Even so, you are likely to continue getting them, unless you try very hard to break the habit of thinking in that way. Say for example you went to the United States and had to drive on the right-hand side ... would that be difficult? Or If you went to a foreign country and had to speak another language, would that be difficult? It usually takes a long time for us to get used to doing something new as automatically as we do something we are used to, but eventually it is possible. People can learn to speak another language as automatically as you speak English, but it takes work, and it takes daily practice.

Change is not always sudden or dramatic. In fact change may depend on how hard you work, but even at best it will be slow. At first your irrational thoughts will be stronger than your counters, but eventually the counters will get stronger, although at times of stress you may have a tendency to revert to your old ways of thinking. Thus it is likely that therapeutic progress will be a series of ups and downs. You may also have noticed that even though some of your negative thinking has changed, you still get negative emotion in some of the old situations.

Voluntary cortical inhibition (VCI)

The technique that you are going to learn now is designed to do two things. First, to help you get rid of the old irrational beliefs or automatic thoughts, and replace them with more rational beliefs, and second to help you get rid of the feeling that has become associated with the various situations.

You did the preparation for VCI last week when you made your hierarchies. You should have those hierarchies on cards in front of you now with the lowest SUDs item on top, the highest SUDs item on the bottom and the others in order in between. You should have a hierarchy for each core belief.

> *Show OHTs 33, 34, and 41. Comment on the essential elements of the hierarchies and answer any questions participants might have.*

Well now that you have completed the preparation for voluntary cortical inhibition, here is how you do it:

> *Show OHT 42 and go through the steps with yourself or a co-therapist demonstrating them.*

Of course at home you don't have to keep rating your SUDs. Simply continue to do steps 2, 3, 5 and 6 until imagining the situation and the negative beliefs disturbs you no more than 10 SUDs, preferably 0.

Voluntary cortical inhibition was also originally described by McMullin and Giles, 1981.

EXERCISE: VOLUNTARY CORTICAL INHIBITION

Do this with two or three scenes, then let participants do a scene or two on their own. Check that they understand what they're doing.

HOMEWORK FOR SESSION TEN

Do either perceptual shift or voluntary cortical inhibition for at least half an hour each day.

• Perceptual shift all Bs.
• Try voluntary cortical inhibition 2–3 times at least.

VCI procedure

1. Relax.

2. Imagine the lowest scene on the hierarchy. (Raise right forefinger when the image is clear.)

3. Think the negative beliefs you would normally think in that situation. (Raise forefinger a second time when situation and beliefs are clearly in mind.)

4. Rate your SUDs level (in the group, by raising your finger when the therapist says the range of SUDs appropriate for you at that time. If SUDs are more than 40 substitute a less threatening item).

5. 'Stop!' (Said by therapist, or say it loudly to yourself.)

6. Argue with your counters strongly and convincingly. (Raise finger when counters are clearly in mind.)

7. Repeat steps 2, 3, 5 and 6 two further times, gradually extending the time between 3 and 5.

8. Repeat 2–4, i.e. obtain SUDs rating without counters. (If SUDs have not decreased consider: were the counters expressed strongly enough, were there sufficient details in the scene, did you argue against the counters, was the countering too indirect, did you counter the wrong beliefs?)

9. Repeat 2–8 until SUDs are 10 or less.

10. Repeat the whole process with the second lowest scene. Continue to move up the hierarchy from least disturbing situation to most disturbing situation.

Figure 14.3. Voluntary cortical inhibition

PROBLEMS THAT MAY ARISE IN SESSION TEN

There are two major problems that can be encountered with perceptual shift: participants being unable see one of the two images that can be seen in the 'old woman/young woman' image, and participants not understanding the process of perceptual shifting. Perceptual shift is made up of two processes: acts of will, and perception. The first act of will is to direct attention to different aspects of the picture, or situation. This leads to a different perception. The different perception can then be reinforced by a second act of will in trying to see different aspects of the picture or situation. When people have difficulty seeing the two images and shifting backwards and forwards from one to the other the therapist can direct the attention of participants to the lines that make up certain aspects of the image as in 'that's the young woman's nose, that's the side of her face, that's a choker round her neck . . .'. The implication is that the participant *tries* to see the lines as the nose of a young woman, the side of her face, and so on. This process is then applied to situations in which participants would normally have negative thoughts: the participant is asked to consider (by an act of will) evidence that supports a positive more general thought (the counter) that is inconsistent with the usual negative thought(s).

There are often two stages in directing one's attention to detailed evidence that supports a counter: the more general summary statement and the evidence for the statement. For example if the counter is 'I am an OK parent' the general summary statement could be 'I often give my children priority over my own interests.' The detailed evidence could be items like 'On Tuesday I turned off the TV news so I could play with Joshua', 'On Wednesday I read to Chantelle when I had been planning to work on my presentation for the following day', 'on Friday we went to McDonalds when I wanted fish and chips.' As with many aspects of this program I have found the best way to help people is to take them through the program one step at a time, with as few distractions as possible. So if the participant has a counter, I will assist them to develop a general summary statement supporting that counter, then assist them to generate one or two items of detailed evidence, then leave them to generate more items of detailed evidence before providing them with positive evidence. The next time I will give them less help.

Conducting voluntary cortical inhibition is fairly difficult in a large group because of the different lengths of time that different people take to relax and to visualise. For this reason the group exercise is only a sample of the procedure when properly applied. The procedure is also fairly complex, and potentially confusing, so it is essential that the therapist leading the exercise is very familiar with the steps and can present it in a clear and seamless way. It may also be necessary to go over the steps a number of times so the participants are also clear on what they have to do.

The other problems encountered with the VCI procedure are the usual ones encountered with systematic desensitisation and other imagery procedures: relaxation-induced anxiety (RAI), and difficulties with imagery, and badly spaced hierarchies. If participants experience RAI, I usually advise them not to use the procedure, and to stick to basic countering or perceptual shift type techniques. However, if the therapist believes strongly that imagery/relaxation techniques will be beneficial, these problems can be dealt with in the usual ways. For relaxation-induced anxiety two approaches can be used. Other relaxation techniques can be used (e.g. isometric relaxation), or the person can be desensitised to relaxation by allowing them to increase tension to a comfortable level and then gradually reduce the tension, getting comfortable with each new level of relaxation before reducing the tension again. If the person is not showing any sign of deconditioning, or if the person is becoming distressed even with the low items on a particular hierarchy, it may be necessary to regenerate the hierarchy, perhaps with lower items and less space between them.

It should be noted that perceptual shift and VCI are not presented as essential, but as examples of a variety of possible approaches which the participant can choose from.

Chapter 15

THERAPY SESSIONS ELEVEN AND TWELVE

GOALS OF SESSION ELEVEN

The goals for Session 11 are straightforward:

1. That participants understand the procedure of self-punishment–self-reward and are able to do it independently.
2. That participants devise a workable plan for themselves that encourages them to continue practising the techniques and approach they have learnt during the program.

In particular, it is hoped that participants will choose one or more maintenance strategies from the set that includes countering, voluntary cortical inhibition, self-punishment–self-reward and the imagery/simulation strategies introduced in this session. It is not essential that a participant use every technique that has been mentioned.

SUMMARY OF SESSION ELEVEN

- Review of homework from previous session
- Lecture A: Self-punishment–self-reward
- Exercise: Self-punishment–self-reward
- Lecture B: Techniques for maintenance
- Exercise: Developing a maintenance plan
- Homework for next week

REVIEW OF HOMEWORK FROM SESSION TEN

1. Perceptual shift
2. Voluntary cortical inhibition

> *Elicit participants' experiences with doing the perceptual shift and voluntary cortical inhibition procedures. Were they easy to apply? What benefits did they experience?*

LECTURE A: SELF-PUNISHMENT–SELF-REWARD

> This is another technique developed by McMullin and Giles, 1981.

We have looked at three methods for changing your thinking: basic countering, perceptual shift, and voluntary cortical inhibition. This fourth approach is called self-punishment–self-reward.

When we want children to do something more often we reward them for doing that thing, and when we want children to do something less often, we punish them for it. We can do the same thing for your thoughts.

We can punish our own negative thinking, and reward positive thinking, which means that we end up thinking more positive thoughts and fewer negative thoughts. The whole thing is done inside your own heads. The instructions are shown in the OHT.

Show OHT 43 (Figure 15.1).

EXERCISE: SELF-PUNISHMENT–SELF-REWARD

Go through self-punishment–self-reward with the group.

LECTURE B: CONTINUED CHANGE

A few sessions ago I mentioned how some people seemed to change their beliefs instantaneously in a 'Eureka' or light-bulb type phenomenon, and some needed to work hard at changing their beliefs, like learning a new skill. It's probably more true that belief change ranges from one extreme to the other: sometimes beliefs change quickly, sometimes they take a long time and lots of work to change, like a bad habit we have had for a long time. Most likely you will have some beliefs that change easily, and some that you have to work on to change.

At the end of this session I am going to suggest that you develop a plan for continued change. We have already looked at four ways of changing your negative beliefs. In a

Write the following on a piece of paper or index card.
1. Pick a negative belief. You can use one of the common negative beliefs, or one of your own.
2. Think of a typical activating event for this belief.
3. What is the *worst possible* consequence of thinking this belief in that situation.
4. What other negative consequences could there be.
5. What is a counter for that belief? (Write on the other side of the card.)
6. What are the *best possible* consequences of thinking and behaving in accordance with the counter belief? What other good consequences might there be? Write them down.

Do this for several beliefs, preferably at least five. Get yourself into a relaxed posture, close your eyes, and rehearse the contents of the cards in your imagination.

Figure 15.1. Self-punishment–self-reward

moment I will present a few others. You can choose from amongst all of these the techniques that you think will be best for you.

Rehearsing the counters

The most basic technique is just to rehearse the counters. You can record your counters on index cards, or on a list in your diary, or as 'wall-paper' on the opening screen of your computer. If you have a few spare minutes you can read them and rehearse them.

Catching yourself using the old false or negative beliefs and countering them

If you notice that you are thinking negative thoughts, you may find the same list or set of cards useful. Again, just take them out and rehearse them in your mind. Later on you may be able to do it without the cards.

Using imagery

Imagery is a useful to practise your counters without waiting for an appropriate activating event. All you do is think of some typical activating events. To use imagery you rehearse typical activating events in your head and practise countering the negative thoughts.

Simulating real situations

Another way to practise using counters is to use simulation. To use simulation you set up situations which are as close as possible to the real thing. You can use imaginary people, or aids such as tape or video or computer recordings, or you can use friends to simulate activating events that are normally associated with negative thinking. You can have a friend role-play your boss, for example.

> This technique is very like 'Stress Inoculation', designed by Meichenbaum, 1974. See other works by Meichenbaum for further details and other ideas for using this strategy.

Using real situations

The most difficult time to use counters is in an unexpected situation. There are two sorts of real situations that you can use to practise for unexpected situations: those you can predict are going to occur, and those you set up. If you know you are going to have a meeting with someone that would usually activate your negative thinking, then make sure you rehearse your counters before you go in so they are much more available for you at the crucial time. Or you can set up the meeting so you can be prepared with your counters, rather than having the meeting sprung on you when you are unprepared.

There are many other ways you can practise thinking rationally and countering negative thoughts. These are simply some of those that I have found to be the most beneficial. The handout gives you references of books you can obtain which will give you more ideas.

Give out handout of Appendix 12 'References for belief change'.

EXERCISE: PLANNING FOR THE FUTURE

1. Make some plans for rehearsal, use of imagery, or simulation, to practise your new beliefs.
2. Decide how you will reward yourself for carrying out these plans.

TERMINATION FUNCTION

> It is often a good idea to have some ritual to finish off the program. Participants will have spent three months in each other's company and may have made significant changes in their lives. There will be a significant gap in their lives when they finish the program. Some might prefer a graduation ceremony with certificates, but I prefer a party. You may even like to have the group decide, which is the thrust of the text below. It is also a time for group members to demonstrate their social competence, so I like to let them do as much of the planning as possible.

You will be aware that next time is the last session in this program. You have now spent 22 hours in each other's company over three months and may have made significant changes in your lives. There will be a significant gap in your lives when you finish the program. We have now finished the content of the course, except for reviewing your plans for continuing and maintaining the changes you have made in your thinking and behaviour as a result of this course, which we will do at the beginning of next session. This gives us most of next session to spend in a suitable way of finishing the course. There are a number of ways this could be done: a little graduation ceremony with certificates, a party here at the clinic at the usual time, a party in the evening or in the weekend at someone's house or some other venue.

> *Facilitate participants in deciding on the kind of function they would like, and in organising it.*

HOMEWORK FOR SESSION ELEVEN

The homework is for participants to complete their maintenance plan as for the exercise.

PROBLEMS THAT MAY ARISE IN SESSION ELEVEN

Few problems are encountered with the content of Session 11. Self-punishment–self-reward is fairly easy for people to grasp, especially after they have dealt with voluntary cortical inhibition. As with VCI it is important for the therapist to have a thorough knowledge of the procedure, so it is presented clearly and seamlessly. Again, it may be helpful to run through the steps a number of times with the group until it is clear that they all understand what they are supposed to do. With devising a maintenance plan it is important to make sure that it is specific, technically correct, and practical. It may also help to reinforce the principles of stimulus control, i.e. by getting them to apply their maintenance plan at regular times and places and/or after specific naturally occurring events in their lives.

There may be difficulties in deciding on the venue and format of the termination function! The therapists may need to use conflict resolution skills to assist the group to come to a consensus regarding the function.

GOALS OF SESSION TWELVE

There are three goals of Session 12: to review the participants' plans for maintaining the gains they made in therapy, to obtain feedback on the program from the participants, and to provide the opportunity for a social closure of the program by means of an appropriate social event.

SUMMARY OF SESSION TWELVE

- Review of homework
- Review of program
- Arrangements for follow-up and post-treatment assessment
- Termination Function

REVIEW OF HOMEWORK FROM SESSION ELEVEN

Homework was to devise a maintenance plan. Try to check participants' plans, perhaps while they are filling out follow-up questionnaires, comment on them, and make suggestions for improvement. Good plans are specific, simple, not overly ambitious, and involve some mechanism to get them going, like having specified times and or dates for the major components.

GROUP DISCUSSION: REVIEW OF THE PROGRAM

Now that you've all completed the program, it's useful to get your ideas about the program. The program is continually evolving, so what you say can help the next group of people. So what I'd like to discuss now is the following five questions:

1. What did you think was good about the group program?
2. What didn't you like about the group program?
3. What did you find useful and what was not useful?
4. What did you find difficult?
5. What aspects of the program do you think should be changed, and what suggestions do you have for change?

Put the five questions, or similar, on a whiteboard or show OHT 44 and encourage discussion. Write the comments down on the board or OHT and keep them for reference. Try to get every participant to make some comments.

ARRANGEMENTS FOR FOLLOW-UP AND POST-TREATMENT ASSESSMENT

There is just one thing left to discuss, and that is follow-up. People have found it useful to meet together after some time is passed to check on progress with the maintenance strategies, to solve any problems that have arisen, and simply to see each other again. These are the approximate times for the follow-up sessions, but I will write to you nearer the time to advise you of the exact date and time.

Put up the approximate dates for the follow-up sessions. You may have different ideas for follow-up and assessment. I think that a schedule of one month, three months, six months and twelve months is good. At these times you can repeat the assessments, check whether the maintenance plans have been adhered to, and problem solve any difficulties that may have occurred.

TERMINATION FUNCTION

Whatever was decided!

PROBLEMS THAT MAY ARISE IN SESSION TWELVE

The only problems that occur in this session are either minor or not very strongly related to cognitive therapy. The problems with maintenance plans include overly ambitious plans or plans without any stimulus control or reinforcement built into them. These can be dealt with by suggestions for modification by the therapist.

The major problem with the evaluation section is that people may not be very forthcoming with negative feedback. The best way to deal with this is for the therapist(s) to present an attitude of concerned self-evaluation throughout the group. If the therapist suspects that negative feedback is being diluted or withheld, then an anonymous written feedback form could be devised, or a third person could be brought in to facilitate the evaluation. Both of these approaches appear to work to some degree.

Part III

Some Final Considerations

Chapter 16

FURTHER DEVELOPMENTS AND FUTURE DIRECTIONS

SUMMARY OF CHAPTER SIXTEEN

- Introduction to the chapter
- Development of this program
- Cut-down cognitive therapy
- One-day cognitive therapy workshop
- Booster sessions
- Process issues

THE FUTURE OF PSYCHOEDUCATIONAL COGNITIVE THERAPY

The factors that led to the development of this program are still relevant, and in most cases still operate. Efficiency of therapy and equity of access continue to be issues. Efficiency and equity of access are integrally related to each other, and to effectiveness. The more efficient a therapy package is, the more people it can be made available to given the same level of resources. Even in the industrialised English-speaking nations access to good quality therapy is still difficult and inequitable. With the advent of economic rationalism fewer services are provided by the state. There are few opportunities for people to access quality psychological therapy at no cost to themselves. Few who have physical access to services can afford the fees charged by private practitioners. Even in developed countries like Australia there are many people suffering from emotional disorders who would not have an available service within several hours travelling time. In westernised countries there are competing lifestyle priorities, which mean that people decide that they cannot afford the money or the time required to complete a program of therapy.

Even if these factors did not continue to operate, there is still a need to improve the effectiveness of cognitive behaviour therapy. The high dropout rate in most studies was noted above. Even the outcome studies with research level resources and highly trained therapists only manage 50–75% success rate for those who complete the study.

Drop-outs and non-completers have been a problem for cognitive behaviour therapy since the earliest efficacy studies. It will be noted from Chapter 3 that there were a number of drop-outs in the evaluation studies of this program, but that they were of the same order as occurred in other outcome studies. Over the years in my private practice a number of people have dropped out of therapy that I believe would have benefited from completing the program. The two main reasons have been competing time demands in their life or a perception that they could not afford to pay for therapy.

These factors were noted in Chapter 1 as providing impetus for improving effectiveness and efficiency of the therapy. They provided the impetus for developing this program, and they have provided the impetus for two further developments: a six-week intense individual psychoeducational program, and an eight-hour one-day workshop group program.

There are numerous ways of improving the effectiveness of therapy and for improving efficiency and equity of access but the ones used in developing this program have been to

- refine the content;
- make the content available in a highly specific manualised form to reduce therapist training and development time;
- run the therapy in groups.

The content of the program presented here has been refined over the years, but the six-session individual psychoeducational program and the one-day workshop are more radical refinements of the basic content. Each of these sets of modifications is discussed below, together with a discussion of the development of this program.

DEVELOPMENT OF THIS PROGRAM

There have a number of changes to the content and the format of the program over the years, though the structure has been much the same. The present program is the result of working from a draft manual, and making changes, either spontaneously during presentation of the material, or after reflection on aspects that participants found difficult. The main change to format that is reflected in the program described in this book is moving from interactive groups of three people helping each other, to the individual work within a classroom model that is presented here. The use of interactive triads meant that fewer examples were completed during sessions. This resulted in less opportunity for each participant to receive feedback and thereby improve the quality of their work. There was also a tendency for the participants in the triads to discuss things other than the task at hand! This was seen as unproductive, but given the lack of knowledge as to what are the active ingredients of therapy it may have been better than doing the exercises. Informal observation suggests that when participants spend a lot of time off task in the group, the overall therapeutic outcome is not as good as in more task-oriented groups.

The major refinements to the content have been in the wording of the text, and the analogies used. I believe that the logic is a lot more cohesive than when I first ran the program, in 1986. For this version of the manual there are few major differences to the manual that was used for the outcome study reported in Chapter 3. There have been some minor changes in the structure to make the workload more evenly distributed across the weeks. Some of the materials used in the draft manuals were copyrighted to other authors, or it was difficult to determine their copyright status. To ensure there were no copyright infringements in the published version any material in which copyright issues were likely to be sensitive was removed. Illustrations were re-drawn, and analogies and metaphors have been recast into an original and parallel form. To the best of my ability, credit has been given within the text by specific citation for any concept or content that is not my own.

Cut-down cognitive therapy

This six-session individual psychoeducational program for cognitive therapy is designed for individual therapy with highly motivated individuals for whom the emotional disorder being treated occurs against a background of excellent pre-morbid functioning. This can either be in the case when the emotional disorder is relatively uncomplicated, or when the cognitive therapy can be delivered as a module within the context of a more inclusive treatment plan. Since the same amount of work has to be done, the patient will have to do more homework, though of course there is the option to spread the Cut-down cognitive therapy (CT) content over more sessions.

Cut-down CT involves the same approach as described in this book, except that all content and exercises not seen as essential are eliminated. I have developed a therapist's manual and a participant's manual for Cut-down CT, but it is possible to use the manual contained in this book simply by leaving out those parts not used in Cut-down CT. The parts of this program used in Cut-down cognitive therapy (CT) are as follows:

- thinking and feeling;
- introduction to the A-B-C model of negative emotion and the three column technique for recording situations that result in negative emotion;
- catching automatic thoughts;
- the suitcase analogy of the process of cognitive therapy;
- Using the vertical arrow approach to identify negative schemas;
- feeling something is true does not mean it is true;
- making a master list of negative beliefs;
- objective analysis;
- logical analysis;
- countering;
- techniques for maintenance.

It can be seen that this program contains all the main elements of CT that have been identified by various researchers, including Jarrett and Nelson (1987). The therapy is presented in a similar format to the group program: the therapist has a manual, presents the introductory material, demonstrates the skill, coaches the client in the session using various examples, assigns homework, and then reviews the homework.

One-day workshop

The one-day workshop is a further development of Cut-down CT. It is not designed as a replacement for the twelve-week program, but is specifically designed for people who have difficulty accessing therapy, either because of the cost, the distance to the therapist, or because of a busy or demanding lifestyle. A one-day workshop can be presented at rural and remote centres, or many people will find it easier to travel to a provincial centre once for a day than once a week for two hours for twelve weeks or more. It may also be good for people who have reservations about psychotherapy, who can receive a taste, and then decide whether or not to continue with individual therapy. It is also possible that the initial workshop could be followed up for people in rural and remote areas by using e-mail, fax or telephone. I have some small experience with the use of e-mail and fax in this way, and it seems to work quite well.

The workshop is delivered in a slightly different format. Although the classroom and individual coaching model is the same as for the group program, the content is given by 'powerpoint' presentation. Participants are provided with workbooks and printouts of the presentation. The main difference is in the material worked on. In the Group Cognitive Therapy program and Cut-down CT there is an attempt to be comprehensive in

Table 16.1. Effect Sizes for the One-day CT Workshop (After Hawgood, 1998)

Beginning of day–end of day

Workshop	Pre-test	Post-test	No. of SDs
Combined	3.04	1.22	1.82
Workshop 1	2.68	1.0	1.68
Workshop 2	3.27	1.37	1.9

Baseline–end of day

Workshop	Pre-test	Post-test	No. of SDs
Combined	3.66	1.22	2.44
Workshop 1	2.84	1.0	1.84
Workshop 2	4.21	1.37	2.84

Note: BDI effect sizes for non-distressed (ND) norms ($M = 4.54$, SD $= 4.46$)

discovering, challenging and changing *all* the client's negative beliefs. In contrast, in the one-day workshop it is assumed that the beliefs discovered, challenged and changed are simply examples to enable the participants to develop the skills, which can then be applied to other beliefs.

Evaluation

Cut-down CRT has not been subjected to any systematic evaluation, though it has been used in a research project that was not concerned with outcome. The One-day Workshop has been evaluated throughout. Hawgood and Free (1999) used a naturalistic design, in which participants' Beck Depression Inventory (BDI) scores were measured at pretest, beginning of day (BOD), end of day (EOD), 1-week follow-up, 1-month follow-up, and 3-month follow-up. 13 persons (4 males and 9 females) participated in the study in two workshops.

The results in Table 16.1 can be compared with the effect sizes shown in Table 3.1. Table 3.1 shows the results for the group CT program compared with the average results for psychological therapy obtained by Free and Oei (1989) in their meta-analysis of some well-known outcome studies. The average change for outcome studies of psychological therapy was 4.02 standard deviation units, and for the group program, 3.717 for the 1987 intake, and 2.46 for the 1992–93 intake. It can be seen that the effect sizes for workshop one (1.84), and workshop two (2.84) in Table 16.1 are quite respectable, especially given the time-limited nature of the treatment.

It is therefore highly likely that this kind of therapy will be made available so that people have a range of formats for cognitive therapy to choose from: standard individual therapy, intense brief individual therapy, medium term (about twelve session) group psychotherapy, and the intensive one-day workshop.

With the advent of briefer cognitive therapies, though, there may be more advantage in 'booster' or 'maintenance' group sessions to assist participants in applying the skills they learnt during the intensive experience. I shall be researching this issue in the near future.

PROCESS ISSUES

The cognitive theory of Beck, Ellis, and McMullin on which this program is based is useful in that it provides the program designer and the therapist with clear guidelines as to what to do in therapy. I have attempted to base this program as much as possible on the consistent theoretical structure outlined in Chapter 2. Even so, it is important to note that evidence that cognitive therapy works for the reasons given by theory is not definitive. In a meta-analytic study, Oei and Free (1995) review the evidence for three of the main process predictions of cognitive theory: does cognitive style change during cognitive therapy, is degree of positive outcome related to the degree of change in negative thinking, and is that change specific to cognitive therapy, or does it occur in other therapies? They conclude that CT does change maladaptive cognitions, but the same positive change in cognitive style occurs in all treatments of depression included in their review, including pharmacological treatment. Positive change in cognitive style even occurs in waiting list control groups, not usually considered to be an active treatment! There was, however, some evidence that the change in negative thinking was less related to changes in depressive symptoms for pharmacological therapy and waiting list than for the so-called 'psychological therapies', but the sample was not sufficient to allow a firm conclusion to be drawn. Thus, according to Oei and Free (1995), it needs to be shown that:

1. The processes of change in cognitive therapy are the active mechanisms in producing the changes in cognitions observed in cognitive therapy.
2. The processes of cognitive therapy specified are the most effective means of producing the change.
3. The change in cognitions is the critical factor in producing remission from depression across all psychological therapies and perhaps even with pharmacotherapy. (p.175)

These are not the only variables of interest, nor are they the only reasons for investigating the processes of therapy. Clearly, if we can determine the active ingredients, then we should be able to improve the efficacy and efficiency and thereby the equity of access of therapy. Many writers have noted that all therapy seems to have similar results. It may therefore be that the active mechanism is another variable such as empathy of the therapist(s).

Clearly it cannot be assumed that any cognitive therapy operates by changing cognitions, let alone that it works by any specified process. It is therefore important to address the process issues in cognitive therapy. The procedures described in this manual, as well as providing a useful set of approaches for working with persons suffering from emotional disorders, also provide the process researcher with a useful and standardised way of conducting therapy whilst studying the processes involved.

Appendices

LIST OF APPENDICES

PHONE SCREENING PROTOCOL

First Name		Surname	
Age		DOB	Gender	
Address			
Phone 1		Phone 2	
What emotional problem?			
How long?			
How much of the time?			

Treatments?	Start	Stop	Who?
Had it before?		When?	

Treatments?	
Head Injury		Alcohol or substance	
First Language		Reading	

INTAKE PROTOCOL

Name:	ID:	Date:	
Inclusion Criteria:			
Major depressive disorder			
Dysthymic disorder			
Adjustment disorder			
Agoraphobia			
Panic disorder			
Social phobia			
Generalised anxiety disorder			
Other appropriate disorder			
Receiving psychological or psychiatric treatment			
Permission obtained from other treating health professional(s)			
Exclusion Criteria:			
Evidence of psychosis			
Acutely suicidal			
Evidence of a comorbid Axis 1 disorder (other than either depression or anxiety disorder)			
Evidence of an Axis 2 (personality) disorder			
People who began a course of medication for depression in the last 3 months			
People who have changed medication for depression in the last 3 months			
First language not English			
Evidence of reading difficulties			
Evidence of brain damage or extensive head injury			

GROUP COGNITIVE THERAPY PROGRAM

Cognitive Therapy is a recognised psychological treatment for emotional disorders such as depression, anxiety disorders and inappropriate anger. It is also used as part of the treatment of a number of behaviour disorders such as alcohol or substance abuse problems and eating disorders.

Cognitive Therapy is based on the idea that emotional disorders can be treated by identifying the false, illogical, and negative thinking that causes and maintains our negative emotions, and by changing it.

This is a group Cognitive Therapy program, but it is not like most people's ideas about group therapy: you don't sit round with a group of strangers discussing your private life. It's more like going back to school. You learn the skills to help you to identify and change your negative thinking in a classroom-like setting.

The groups are held weekly. Each weekly two-hour session consists of mini-lectures and exercises. In the mini-lectures the group leader explains and demonstrates a skill. In the exercises you apply the skill to your own situation with assistance from the therapist(s).

Homework is a very important part of the program. Once you have learnt the skill with the assistance of the therapists, it is expected that you will go home and work on other aspects of your thinking in your own time. If you have difficulty with the homework, the therapist will help you with it in the next session. Most people find that about five to six hours of homework are required each week.

AN INTRODUCTION TO COGNITIVE THERAPY

Prior to the incorporation of cognitive therapy in the late 1970s, behaviour therapy was limited to approaches derived from operant conditioning and classical conditioning. These were very effective with a number of emotional and behavioural problems: simple phobias, assertiveness problems, and skill deficits. Behaviour modification was useful in reducing frequency of negative behaviour in people with intellectual deficits and helped teachers and parents develop effective behaviour management. Despite this success in some areas, there were difficulties in applying the approach to anxiety states and depression.

At this time depression was seen by behavioural psychologists as a skills deficit, or a deficiency in reinforcement, and anxiety states were treated with relaxation, or as a collection of phobias using an exposure based intervention.

None of these approaches was entirely satisfactory. The behavioural theories did not seem to explain depression adequately. Relaxation on its own was a rather weak treatment, and constructing the multiple hierarchies necessary to treat generalised anxiety was difficult and time consuming. A new generation of was beginning to dispute the wisdom of not allowing any credibility for cognitive phenomena in the understanding of the motives and functioning of human beings. They thought that the flow of verbal language and imagery that passes through our awareness must have some impact on our emotional functioning.

In the 1960s a number of clinicians became aware of these problems and proposed theories of emotional disturbance based on distorted thinking and developed treatment packages accordingly.

Two of the most influential in terms of acceptance of their theories and treatment were **Albert Ellis** and **Aaron Beck**. Ellis taught three major "insights". In insight number one, the individual realises that he or she has a problem that has a specific cause or causes. In insight number two the person realises that certain irrational beliefs acquired in childhood, which occur between an activating event and an emotional consequence, are causing his or her emotional upset. In insight number three the person understands that he or she must work hard to change those negative patterns of thinking.

Ellis' notions of what constitutes irrational thinking have changed over the years. In the early stages he focussed on "absolutist" thinking, in which the thought concerns an extreme such as "perfection", or "never" (as in "I will never be any good"), or deals with phenomena as if they were dichotomous rather than relative.

Beck taught that thinking could be faulty in three different ways: the structure of thinking, the content of thinking, and the process of thinking. Two types of thinking are part of the **structural** aspect of Beck's theory: automatic thoughts, and schemas or core beliefs. **Automatic thoughts** are transient, are very quick and telegraphic in nature, and are part of the stream of consciousness. They occur at the surface of consciousness but are not part of our directed control. **Schemas** are more permanent structures that result from the interpretation of developmental experiences. Schemas are the templates that we use to react to events in our day to day lives. The **content** of both automatic thoughts and schemas can be nonadaptive in three areas, known as the "Cognitive Triad". The **cognitive triad** consists of negative thinking about the **self**, the **world**, and the **future**.

The **process** of thinking can be distorted in a number of ways. Two examples are **Dichotomous Thinking** and **Personalization**. With **Dichotomous Thinking** if a thing or person is not perfect, it is no good. **Personalization** involves cognitively taking total responsibility for an event that one may have only partially contributed to the outcome of.

Beck's theory was originally applied to depression, anxiety, and anger, but has since been applied to personality disorders. For the moment we will consider how depression may develop. As shown in the diagram on the next page, a person may have a set of negative experiences in childhood, or experiences that lead to the negative schema "I am worthless", or the conditional negative schema "I am worthless if I fail to achieve". They may also develop faulty patterns of logic. The negative schemas and faulty patterns of logic constitute a vulnerability to depression. Later in life the person may experience a negative event consistent with the vulnerability, such as an achievement event. The event is interpreted negatively using faulty logic: "I didn't achieve a perfect result, therefore the result is bad". This faulty

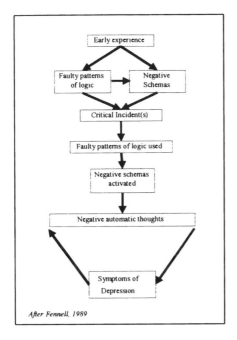

After Fennell, 1989

(Figure boxes: Early experience → Faulty patterns of logic / Negative Schemas → Critical Incident(s) → Faulty patterns of logic used → Negative schemas activated → Negative automatic thoughts → Symptoms of Depression)

logic activates the negative schema: "Therefore I am worthless", which may lead to or maintain depression by virtue of frequent negative automatic thoughts.

Cognitive therapy seeks to undo this process and thereby alleviate the symptoms of depression, first by reducing the frequency of negative automatic thoughts, and second by reducing the vulnerability associated with negative schemas. There are four major steps in the process: identifying the person's negative automatic thoughts, schemas, and faulty thought processes; achieving a comprehensive understanding of the person's cognitive structure; challenging and eventually changing critical aspects of that cognitive structure; and developing strategies to maintain the new ways of thinking. The process has been well described for depression (eg. Beck, Rush, Shaw & Emery, 1979), anxiety disorders, and to a lesser degree for personality disorders (Beck, Freeman and Associates, 1990)

The therapy has also been extensively evaluated, including in comparison to biological therapies. It seems that the therapy does not differ in effectiveness from antidepressant medication, and may have slightly superior results over the long-term, though different reviewers come to different conclusions (eg. Free and Oei, 1989)

It should not be concluded that the effectiveness of the therapy definitively supports the cognitive theory of depression, nor even that negative thinking is seen as the sole or primary factor in the aetiology and maintenance of depression. Beck is quite clear that he sees depression as an interaction of cognitive, behavioural, and biological processes. Cognitive therapy is just one way of intervening in the complex set of processes that comprise the emotional disorders. In support of intervening in multiple modalities, Free & Oei (1989) conclude from their meta-analysis that the treatment of choice is a combination of cognitive therapy and antidepressant medication.

References and Suggested Reading

Beck, A.T. (1987). Cognitive models of depression. *Journal of Cognitive Psychotherapy, An International Quarterly,* 1, 5–37.

Beck, A. T., Rush, A.J., Shaw, B.F., & Emery, G. (1979). *Cognitive therapy of depression.* New York: The Guilford Press.

Beck, A.T. (1976). *Cognitive therapy and the emotional disorders.* New York: International Universities Press.

Beck, A.T., Freeman, A., & Associates. (1990) *Cognitive Therapy of the Personality Disorders.* New York: The Guilford Press.

Burns, D.D. (1980). *Feeling Good: The new mood therapy.* New York: Signet.

Ellis, A., & Harper, R. A. (1975). *A new guide to rational living.* Englewood Cliffs, NJ: Wilshire.

Free, M.L., & Oei, T.P. (1989). Biological and psychological processes in the treatment and maintenance of depression. *Clinical Psychology Review, 9,* 653–688.

Michael Free PhD

HOMEWORK CONTRACT

I . . . .(Name)

Contract with myself to do my cognitive therapy homework at the times indicated below

Monday   . . . .

Tuesday   . . . .

Wednesday   . . . .

Thursday   . . . .

Friday   . . . .

Saturday   . . . .

Sunday   . . . .

Every week I spend 80% or more of the target time on my homework, eg 4 or more hours out of 5 I will reward myself with:

. . . .

Signed . . . .   **Date** . . . .

Appendix 6

OVERHEAD PROJECTOR
TRANSPARENCY MASTERS

OHT 1   THE THREE SYSTEMS MODEL

thinking

behaviour

emotion

physiology

OHT 2   THE A-B-C SEQUENCE

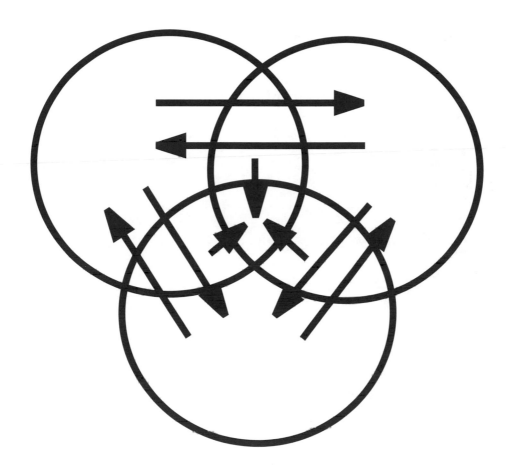

OHT 3   REFEREE WHISTLING

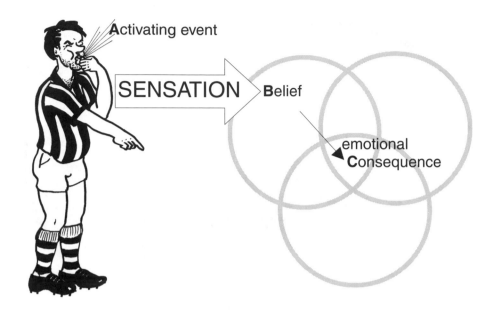

('Referee' by V. Parslow-Stafford)

OHT 4   THE THREE-COLUMN APPROACH (WOLF-SHADOW ETC.)

The Three Column Approach (1)

Activating event	Belief or thought	emotional Consequence
Shadow of dressing gown	That's a wolf and it's going to eat me	Fear
	That's just the shadow of the dressing gown	None

Activating event	Belief or thought	emotional Consequence
Overate and feel sick	I've got food poisoning. I might die	Fear
	I ate too much rich food	None

OHT 5   THREE-COLUMN EXAMPLES: PARTY, VASE

The Three Column Approach (2)

Activating event	Belief or thought	emotional Consequence
Going to a party	I might not be able to think of anything to say	anxious
	I might have an interesting time	excited

Activating event	Belief or thought	emotional Consequence
Broke a vase	I never really liked it	pleased
	That was my favourite reminder of Aunt Betty	sad

OHT 6   THREE-COLUMN EXAMPLES: BOSS, SPEECH

The Three Column Approach (3)

Activating event	Belief or thought	emotional Consequence
Boss yells	That swine has a nerve...	anger
	I'm useless	depression

Activating event	Belief or thought	emotional Consequence
Giving a speech and audience member walks out		

OHT 7   THREE-COLUMN EXAMPLES: PASS BY, DEPRESSION

The Three Column Approach (4)

Activating event	Belief or thought	emotional Consequence
Acquaintance passes you by without acknowledgement		

Activating event	Belief or thought	emotional Consequence
Wake in the morning feeling depressed		*More depressed*
		Less depressed

OHT 8   THREE-COLUMN BLANK

Three Column Form

Activating event	Belief or thought	emotional Consequence

OHT 9   THE SAINT/CHECKLIST

('Saint' by V. Parslow-Stafford; 'Checklist' by R. Allen; halo and thought bubble from IMSI's MasterClips Collection, 1895 Francisco Blvd. East, San Rafael, CA 94901-5506, USA)

OHT 10   THE SUITCASE ANALOGY

('Suitcase' by R. Allen)

OHT 11   AUTOMATIC THOUGHTS (1)

Characteristics of Automatic Thoughts

- They are short and specific.

- They occur extremely rapidly, immediately after the event.

- They do not occur in sentences, but may consist of a few key words or images.

- They do not arise from careful thought.

- They do not occur in a logical series of steps such as in problem solving.

- They seem to happen just by reflex.

Adapted from Beck et al. (1979)

OHT 12   AUTOMATIC THOUGHTS (2)

Characteristics of Automatic Thoughts (2)

- You do not summon them up, and you can't send them away.

- They seem reasonable at the time.

- Often a person will have automatic thoughts with the same theme.

- People with the same emotional problem have the same kind of automatic thoughts.

- Automatic thoughts involve more distortion of reality than other types of thinking.

Adapted from Beck et al. (1979)

Common Negative Beliefs/Schemas (1)

- **I Stink**   I am worthless, no good, of no value.

- **You Stink**   A person who offends me is no good, a total bastard.

- **Namby-Pamby**   I can't stand it, I can't cope, I'll go crazy.

- **Monster** I am coming to harm, I am sick.

- **Doomsday**   This event is catastrophic, the future is hopeless.

- **Fairy-tale**   **Things should be better; the world should be like x.**

(after McMullin and Casey, 1977)

OHT 14   TYPES OF NEGATIVE BELIEFS/SCHEMAS (2)

Common Negative Beliefs/Schemas (2)

- **Alone**   I am rejected, I am alone.

- **Kitten**   I am powerless.

- **Bomb**   I am out of control.

- **Victim**   It is unfair. The World/Fate/God/Cosmos has done me wrong.

Logical Errors (1)

Extreme Thinking
- *Going beyond the facts*
  - More dire than justified
  - False Absolutes
  - Faulty prediction
  - Invalid allocation of responsibility
  - Unjustified conclusions about motive or opinion
- *Misinterpreting the facts*
  - Biased weighting
- *Not considering all the facts*
- *Using only dichotomous categories*
- *Rating things that are unrateable*

Arbitrary Thinking
- *Shoulds*
- *Using emotion to verify belief*

OHT 16   LOGICAL ERRORS (2)

Logical Errors (2)

Going beyond the facts

- **More dire than justified:** You conclude a situation is worse than it really is.
- **False Absolutes:** You use absolute words such as 'never', 'always', 'everyone', and 'everything' when inconsistent events or situations are possible, if not probable.
- **Faulty prediction:** You predict that things will turn out worse than is likely when all relevant information is considered.
- **Invalid allocation of responsibility:** Allocating disproportionate amounts of responsibility for negative events either on yourself or a significant other person
- **Unjustified conclusions about motive or opinion:** Concluding you know the reason for a person's behaviour or their opinion of you, when you do not have access to the full set of the persons reasons, drives, and motives.

Logical Errors (3)

- **Misinterpreting the facts:** You consider all the facts, but you misinterpret them. One form is *Biased weighting,* in which you bias the information relating to one situation or person, or coming from one source positively or negatively.
- **Not considering all the facts:** You select only the facts which support one conclusion, usually the negative conclusion
- **Using only dichotomous categories:** Otherwise known as dichotomous thinking or black and white thinking. You polarise judgements: a person, situation, event, or outcome is either totally good or totally bad.
- **Rating the unrateable:** You attempt to rate something like the value of a person when there is no reasonable *single* standard or scale against which to rate the thing.

Logical Errors (4)

Arbitrary Thinking

You make statements that have no basis in fact, that are divorced from any evidence to support them.

- **'Should' Statements**: You arbitrarily specify that certain events are to happen or are to happen under certain circumstances, when there is no process to cause them to happen

- **Using emotion to verify belief**: concluding that a person, event, situation or outcome has a certain attribute because it *feels* that way.

Catching Automatic Thoughts

1. Know the characteristics of Automatic Thoughts.

2. Look for their tracks, ie the emotion they leave behind.

3. Know their habits and be on the lookout.

4. Set traps.

5. Trick them with your imagination.

OHT 20   THE OCEAN ANOLOGY

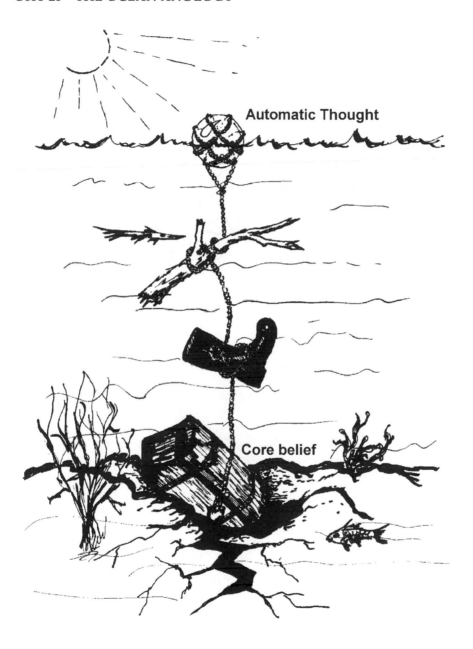

('Ocean Analogy' by V. Parslow-Stafford)

OHT 21   THE BULB-NET ANALOGY

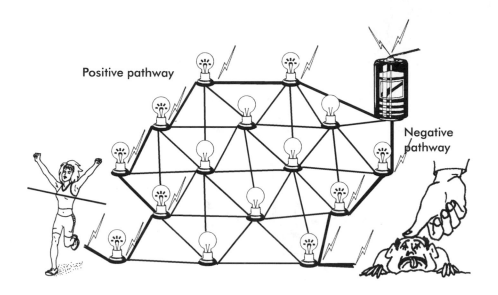

('Winner' and 'Thumb' by V. Parslow-Stafford. Other elements from IMSI's MasterClips Collection, 1895 Francisco Blvd. East, San Rafael, CA 94901-5506, USA)

OHT 22   THE FOOTBALLER VERTICAL ARROW

We lost again!
↓
It was my fault!
↓
I'll never be any good!
↓
I'm a waste of space!

('Footballer' by V. Parslow-Stafford)

OHT 23   THE REFEREE VERTICAL ARROW

That wasn't a foul!

↓

That ref is biased!

↓

He shouldn't be reffing

↓

He's hopeless!

('Referee' by V. Parslow-Stafford)

OHT 24   HOUSEWORK VERTICAL ARROW

Vertical Arrow
Example 3

A: Doing the housework

C: Anxious

B1 I want everything to be spotless
otherwise people will think I'm dirty and
untidy

↓

B2 People would think badly of me

↓

B3 I will be unwanted and neglected

↓

B4 I am useless and a nobody

↓

B5 Nobody will want to love me

↓

B6 I will always be alone

↓

B7 I am unwanted

↓

B8 I will always be unhappy

Basic Instructions for the Vertical Arrow Procedure

1. Follow the negative associations by asking the questions:

    'If _____ is true, what would that mean to me?' or

    'If _____ is true, why would that be so bad?'

2. Concentrate on one emotion at a time.

3. Work from specifics to generalisations.

4. Search for core meaning of statements.

5. Avoid descriptions of feeling.

6. Avoid questions "Why is he/she ..."

7. Avoid statements of desire "I wish ..."

OHT 26   ADVANCED VERTICAL ARROW INSTRUCTIONS

Advanced Instructions for the Vertical Arrow Procedure

1. Focus on key words.
2. Imagine the situation as vividly as you can.
3. Be aware of images associated with each belief: visual, auditory, kinaesthetic.
4. Investigate the meaning of the statement in terms of your life history.
5. Specify both halves of conditional sentences, the meaning of pronouns, all parts of the sentence, the exact people, all probabilities.
6. Check that the emotion associated with the belief intensifies as you go down the Vertical Arrow.
7. When unable to go further ask yourself the more specific questions: If this was true, what would it mean about...me as a person? the world? my future?
8. Core beliefs, which come at the bottom of the Vertical Arrows, can be recognised by their general and absolute nature.
9. Or take the form of one of the common negative beliefs or schemas.

OHT 27   EXAMPLES OF MASTER LIST OF BELIEFS (1)

Type of belief:	*Core*
I am worthless	
I am helpless	
I am a coward	
I am unloved	
I am alone	
I am a failure	

Type of belief:	*Conditional*
If he leaves me I will be alone	
I would be worthless if he left me	
I am an ineffective parent if my son misbehaves	
If he leaves me I am not good enough to hold a man	
If my children don't love me nobody will	
If he leaves I'll never be able to face people again	

OHT 28   EXAMPLES OF MASTER LIST OF BELIEFS (2)

Type of belief:	*Core*
I will always be alone	
I'm a real failure	
My life is a mess	
I will never be loved	
I'm a terrible person	
Being alone is awful	
I'm stupid	

Type of belief:	*Conditional*
If I make mistakes people will think I'm stupid	
I will go crazy if I have a panic attack	
If I go crazy I will be locked up and never get out	
If I go crazy I am weak	

OHT 29   EXAMPLES OF MASTER LIST OF BELIEFS (3)

Type of belief:	*Specific*
He doesn't love me	
I am a bad parent	
People think I am stupid	
He only touches me when he wants something	
I need people to like me	
I am an embarrassment to people	
People think I am a rotten person	
He is always trying to get away from me	
He is using me	

OHT 30   EXAMPLES OF COGNITIVE MAPS (1)

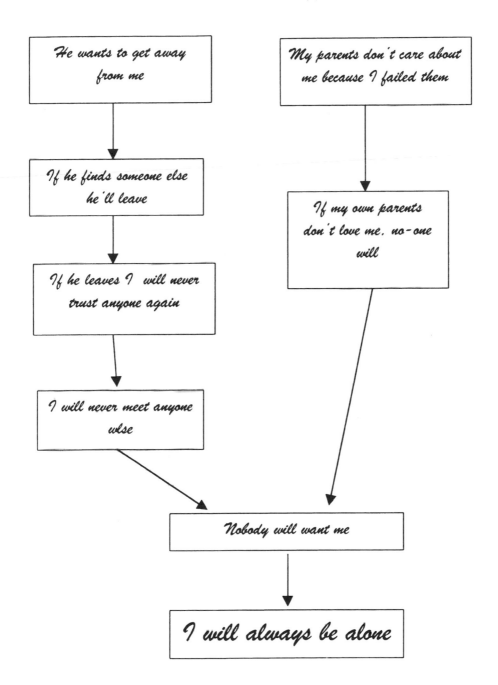

OHT 31   EXAMPLES OF COGNITIVE MAPS (2)

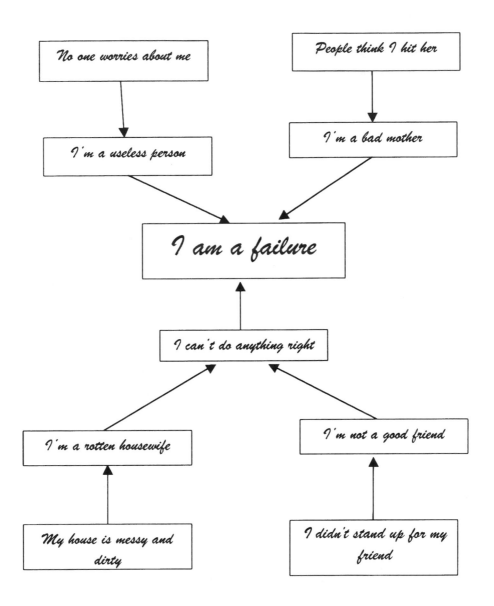

OHT 32   EXAMPLES OF COGNITIVE MAPS (3)

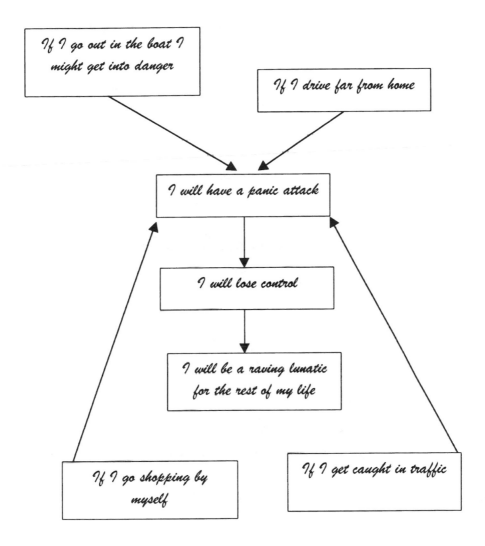

OHT 33 EXAMPLES OF HIERARCHIES (1)

Theme:	*Failure*
SUDS	**Item**
100	Hurting my child very badly
95	
90	Having a child go to prison
85	Have a child go to court
80	My husband leaving me
75	
70	My husband going on holiday without me
65	Having a car accident that is my fault
60	The house being untidy
55	Forgetting my best friend's birthday
50	
45	Buying something expensive that turns out to be useless
40	
35	Forgetting the house payment
30	
25	Losing my wallet
20	Ruining a meal
15	Breaking a glass
10	
5	Dropping food on the floor

OHT 34   EXAMPLES OF HIERARCHIES (2)

Theme:	*Losing Control: Having a panic attack in*
SUDS	**Item**
100	*An aeroplane over the sea*
95	
90	*An aeroplane over desert*
85	
80	*An aeroplane over populated areas*
75	*In a boat on the bay with a work colleague*
70	
65	*In a boat on the bay with my son-in-law*
60	
55	*In a boat on the bay with my best friend*
50	*In a train*
45	*In a traffic jam*
40	
35	*In traffic*
30	*2 km from home on foot*
25	
20	*A lift*
15	*1 km from home on foot*
10	
5	*At home with my partner*

The Definition of a Counter

A counter is a thought which argues against another thought and includes such activities as thinking or behaving in the opposite direction, arguing in a very assertive fashion, and convincing oneself of the falsity of a belief.

(McMullin & Giles, 1981, p. 65)

OHT 36   RULES OF COUNTERING

The Rules of Countering

1. Counters must be directly opposite to the false belief.
2. A counter must be a believable statement of reality.
3. Develop as many counters as possible for each belief.
4. The counters must be your own.
5. Counters must be concise.
6. Counters must be stated with assertive intensity.
7. Counters should be as strong as possible.

(McMullin & Giles, 1981, pp. 67–68; reproduced by permission of Grune & Stratton Inc.)

OHT 37   THE PROCESS OF COUNTERING

Unmodified negative thinking

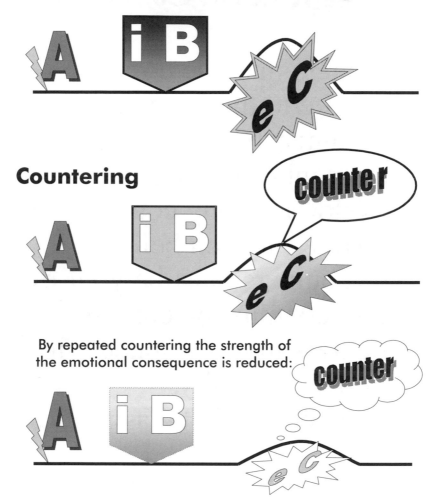

Countering

By repeated countering the strength of
the emotional consequence is reduced:

Eventually the irrational belief is replaced by
a rational belief (rB) and no emotional consequence occurs

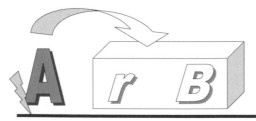

('Countering' by V. Parslow-Stafford)

Countering using index cards

On one side write the irrational belief:

> *I am worthless*

And on the other write the counter:

> *I am worthwhile because all people are worthwhile*

OHT 39   PICTURE OF OLD/YOUNG WOMAN

OHT 40   PERCEPTUAL SHIFT USING INDEX CARDS

Perceptual Shift using index cards

On one side write the irrational belief:

> *I am worthless*

And on the other write the counter and evidence:

> *I am worthwhile because all people are worthwhile*
> *My society values all people, because*
> *There is punishment for murder and physical harm*
> *People unable to care for themselves are cared for*
> *I value all other people for who they are. I don't ask them to do anything to be valued by me*
> *My religion tells me that all people are worthwhile and to be valued*
> *I choose to continue to be a person*

OHT 41   VOLUNTARY CORTICAL INHIBITION (1)

Voluntary Cortical Inhibition: Preparation

- Have a hierarchy for each cluster or beliefs.
- Print each situation on an index card, together with negative thoughts and counters.

OHT 42   VOLUNTARY CORTICAL INHIBITION (2)

Voluntary Cortical Inhibition: Procedure

1. Relax.
2. Imagine the lowest scene on the hierarchy (raise right forefinger when the image is clear).
3. Think the negative beliefs you would normally think in that situation (raise forefinger again when situation and beliefs are clearly in mind).
4. Rate your SUDs level. If SUDs are more than 40 substitute a less threatening item.
5. 'Stop!' (said by therapist, or say it loudly to yourself).
6. Argue with your counters strongly and convincingly (raise finger when counters are clearly in mind).
7. Repeat steps 2, 3, 5 and 6 two further times, gradually extending the time between 3 and 5.
8. Repeat 2–4, i.e. obtain SUDs rating without counters.
9. Repeat 2–8 until SUDs are 10 or less.
10. Repeat the whole process with the second lowest scene.

Continue to move up the hierarchy from least disturbing situation to most disturbing situation.

Self-Punishment–Self-Reward

1. Pick a negative belief. You can use one of the common negative beliefs, or one of your own.

2. Think of a typical activating event for this belief.

3. What is *worst possible* consequence of thinking this belief in that situation?

4. What other negative consequences could there be?

Write all that on a piece of paper or index card.

5. What is a counter for that belief? (Write on the other side of the card.)

6. What are the *best possible* consequences of thinking and behaving in accordance with the counter belief? What other good consequences might there be? Write them down.

Do this for several beliefs, preferably at least five. Get yourself into a relaxed posture, close your eyes, and rehearse the contents of the cards in your imagination.

OHT 44   EVALUATION QUESTIONS

Questions for Feedback from Participants

1. What you thought was good about the group cognitive therapy program;

2. What you didn't like about the group cognitive therapy program;

3. What you found useful and what was not useful;

4. What you found difficult;

5. What aspects of the program you think should be changed, and suggestions for change.

Appendix 7

MASTER LIST OF BELIEFS

(Core/conditional/specific to situation)

Type of Belief:

Belief		Analyses								
		Objective	Utility				Consistency			Logical
	Belief Category	(T=true, F=false)	Feel better (Y=yes, N=no)	Achieve goals (Y=yes, N=no)	Better with others (Y=yes, N=no)	(UF=useful, UL=useless)	Self (Y=yes, N=no)	Others (Y=yes, N=no)	(T=true, F=false)	(T=true, F=false)

Appendix 8

EXAMPLES OF LOGICAL ANALYSIS

CATASTROPHE

Original belief. Write your original belief as it appears on your master list of beliefs.

It would be awful and catastrophic if she left me.

Analysable belief State the principle or relationship that underlies the belief. State it in an analysable form. State all parts of the sentence. Be specific. Avoid pronouns and general terms.

It would be awful and catastrophic if my partner left me

Define your terms. Identify all key words. Define them as concretely as possible. Use a dictionary if necessary, but define the terms the way you meant them when you had the thought. Specify the levels of probability.

Key word	Definition
awful	*solemnly impressive; ultimately bad*
catastrophe	*event subverting system of things; sudden or widespread noteworthy disaster*

Rewrite sentence: *It would be the end of all things if my partner left me.*

Decide your rules. What information would prove your belief false? What information would prove it true?

False if:	*I could survive and function, however difficult it was, if my partner left me*
True if:	*There is no other way I could function than with my present partner.*

Find and examine your evidence. How do you plan to get your evidence: using your senses, asking an authority, using your own experience, using reason and logic, finding what the majority think, setting up an experiment?

Plan:	*Use my own experience. Have I been able to function without this partner in the past. Has there been any change that would make this impossible?*

What specific evidence would you accept? (e.g. False if 4 out 5 experts say)

False if:	*I have been able to function without this partner and conditions are generally the same*
True if:	*This partner is essential to my functioning*

Stating your verdict

The evidence was:	*I was able to function before I met my partner. I function when she is away*
Therefore the belief is:	*False*

APPEASEMENT

Original belief. Write your original belief as it appears on your master list of beliefs.
I must appease people who are angry
Analysable belief State the principle or relationship that underlies the belief. State it in an analysable form. State all parts of the sentence. Be specific. Avoid pronouns and general terms.
People who are angry will cause me harm if I don't appease them.
Define your terms. Identify all key words. Define them as concretely as possible. Use a dictionary if necessary, but define the terms the way you meant them when you had the thought. Specify the levels of probability.

Key word	Definition
Angry	*showing nonverbal signs of anger*
will cause	*80% probability*
harm	*hurt as a consequence of a deliberate act*
appease	*give in or compromise*

Rewrite sentence:
8 out of 10 times, if I don't give in or compromise to people displaying nonverbal sign of anger, they will deliberately hurt me.
Decide your rules. What information would prove your belief false? What information would prove it true?

False if:	*On more than 20% of occasions when I don't give in or compromise, the person does not deliberately try to hurt me*
True if:	*If the person does try to harm me*

Find and examine your evidence. How do you plan to get your evidence: using your senses, asking an authority, using your own experience, using reason and logic, finding what the majority think, setting up an experiment?
Plan:
Use my own experience. Keep a diary, record incidents when I don't give in or compromise. Note whether the other person deliberately tries to hurt me.

False if:	*as above*

Stating your verdict

The evidence was:	*No one tried to hurt me in more than 10 incidents when I did not give in or compromise*

Therefore the belief is:	*False*

ALONE

Original belief. Write your original belief as it appears on your master list of beliefs. *I am alone*
Analysable belief State the principle or relationship that underlies the belief. State it in an analysable form. State all parts of the sentence. Be specific. Avoid pronouns and general terms.
Define your terms. Identify all key words. Define them as concretely as possible. Use a dictionary if necessary, but define the terms the way you meant them when you had the thought. Specify the levels of probability.

Key word	Definition
alone	*do not have a single person to have a relationship with.*
relationship	*able to share confidences and feelings without fear of rejection.*
Rewrite sentence:	*I do not have a person with whom I can share confidences without fear of rejection.*

Decide your rules. What information would prove your belief false? What information would prove it true?

False if:	*I know, or can find a person with whom I can share confidences and talk about feelings with and I am not rejected.*
True if:	*After searching for a reasonable length of time I have not found such a person*

Find and examine your evidence. How do you plan to get your evidence: using your senses, asking an authority, using your own experience, using reason and logic, finding what the majority think, setting up an experiment?
Plan:
Over six months target 10 people and share confidences and feelings with them.

What specific evidence would you accept? (e.g. False if 4 out of 5 experts say …)	
False if:	*Even one does not reject me*
True if:	*They all reject me.*

Stating your verdict
The evidence was:
Therefore the belief is:

WORTHLESS

Original belief. Write your original belief as it appears on your master list of beliefs. *I am worthless*
Analysable belief. State the principle or relationship that underlies the belief. State it in an analysable form. State all parts of the sentence. Be specific. Avoid pronouns and general terms. *I do not serve any useful purpose*

Define your terms. Identify all key words. Define them as concretely as possible. Use a dictionary if necessary, but define the terms the way you meant them when you had the thought. Specify the levels of probability.

Key word	Definition
useful	*able to produce a good result*
purpose	*goal, good result of benefit to people*

Rewrite sentence: *I am unable to produce a good result which is of benefit to people, and am therefore of no value*

Decide your rules. What information would prove your belief false? What information would prove it true?

False if:	*A person can be of value even if they are unable to produce a good result.*
True if:	*A person is automatically valueless if he or she cannot produce results that benefit others.*

Find and examine your evidence. How do you plan to get your evidence: using your senses, asking an authority, using your own experience, using reason and logic, finding what the majority think, setting up an experiment?

Plan:	*Find out what others think.*

What specific evidence would you accept? (e.g. False if 4 out 5 experts say ...)

False if:	*Nine out of ten people say that a person can have value even if they do not benefit others, eg. profoundly handicapped people.*
True if:	*Two or more out of ten say a person can't have value.*

Stating your verdict

The evidence was	*Ten out ten people asked said a person could have value even if he or she did not benefit others*
Therefore the belief is:	*False*

WHO'S WHO

Original belief. Write your original belief as it appears on your master list of beliefs.

I must be perfect to succeed in life.

Analysable belief State the principle or relationship that underlies the belief. State it in an analysable form. State all parts of the sentence. Be specific. Avoid pronouns and general terms.

It is necessary to be perfect to be successful.

Define your terms. Identify all key words. Define them as concretely as possible. Use a dictionary if necessary, but define the terms the way you meant them when you had the thought. Specify the levels of probability.

Key word	Definition
Perfect	*Without blemish or fault*
Success	*listed in "Who's Who".*

Rewrite sentence: *It is necessary to be without blemish or fault to be listed in Who's Who.*

Decide your rules. What information would prove your belief false? What information would prove it true?

False if:	*Even one person in "Who's Who" can be shown to have a blemish or fault*
True if:	*Not one person in "Who's Who" can be found to have a blemish or fault.*

Find and examine your evidence. How do you plan to get your evidence: using your senses, asking an authority, using your own experience, using reason and logic, finding what the majority think, setting up an experiment?

Plan:

Consult "Who's Who", biographies, newspapers, magazines.

What specific evidence would you accept? (e.g. False if 4 out 5 experts say ...)

False if:	*There is evidence that at least one person listed in "Who's Who" has blemishes or faults.*

Stating your verdict

The evidence was	*Many people in "Who's Who" had blemishes or faults.*
Therefore the belief is:	*False*

LOGICAL ANALYSIS WORKSHEET

Original belief. Write your original belief as it appears on your master list of beliefs.

Analysable belief
State the principle or relationship that underlies the belief. State it in an analysable form. State all parts of the sentence. Be specific. Avoid pronouns and general terms.

Define your terms. Identify all key words. Define them as concretely as possible. Use a dictionary if necessary, but define the terms the way you meant them when you had the thought. Specify the levels of probability.

Key word	Definition

Rewrite sentence:

Decide your rules. What information would prove your belief false? What information would prove it true?

False if:

True if:

Find and examine your evidence. How do you plan to get your evidence: using your senses, asking an authority, using your own experience, using reason and logic, finding what the majority think, setting up an experiment?

Plan:

What specific evidence would you accept? (e.g. False if 4 out 5 experts say ...)

False if:

True if:

Stating your verdict

The evidence was:

Therefore the belief is:

FOUR COLUMN CHART (PERCEPTUAL SHIFT)

Situation:

Irrational Thoughts	T/F	Counter	Evidence

NEGATIVE EMOTION CHART (HIERARCHY FORM)

Theme:	
SUDS	Item
100	
95	
90	
85	
80	
75	
70	
65	
60	
55	
50	
45	
40	
35	
30	
25	
20	
15	
10	
5	

Appendix 12

REFERENCES FOR BELIEF CHANGE

Burns, DD (1980) *Feeling Good: The new mood therapy* New York: Signet

Ellis, A, & Harper, RA (1975) *A new guide to rational living* Englewood Cliffs, NJ: Wilshire

McMullin, RE (1986) *Handbook of cognitive therapy techniques* New York: WW Norton and Company

McMullin, RE (1999) *The new handbook of cognitive therapy techniques* New York: WW Norton and Company

REFERENCES

Abramson, LY, Metalsky, GI, and Alloy, LB (1989) Hopelessness depression: A theory based subtype of depression *Psychological Review*, **96**, 358–372

Abramson, LY, Seligman, MEP, and Teasdale, JD (1978) Learned helplessness in humans: critique and reformulation *Journal of Abnormal Psychology*, **87**, 49–74

American Psychiatric Association (1987) *Diagnostic and statistical manual of mental disorders* (3rd edn revised) Washington, DC

American Psychiatric Association (1993) *Diagnostic and statistical manual of mental disorders* (4th edn) Washington, DC

American Psychological Association (1993, October) *Final Report of the Task Force on Promotion and Dissemination of Psychological Procedures* New York: American Psychological Association, Division of Clinical Psychologists (Division 12)

Barber, JP and DeRubeis, RJ (1989) On second thought: Where the action is in cognitive therapy for depression *Cognitive Therapy and Research*, **13**, 441–457

Barlow, DH (Ed.) (1993) *Clinical Handbook of Psychological Disorders: A step-by-step treatment manual* (2nd edn) New York: The Guilford Press

Beck, AT (1976) *Cognitive therapy and the emotional disorders* New York: International Universities Press

Beck, AT (1987) Cognitive models of depression *Journal of Cognitive Psychotherapy, An International Quarterly*, **1**, 5–37

Beck, AT, Brown, G, Steer, RA, and Weissman, AN (1991) Factor analysis of the dysfunctional attitude scale in a clinical population *Psychological Assessment*, **3**, 478–483

Beck, AT and Emery, G (1985) *Anxiety disorders and phobias: A cognitive perspective* New York: Basic Books

Beck, AT, Freeman, A, and Associates (1990) *Cognitive Therapy of the Personality Disorders* New York: The Guilford Press

Beck, AT, Hollon, SD, Young, JE, Bedrosian, RC, and Budenz, D (1985) Treatment of depression with cognitive therapy and amitriptyline *Archives of General Psychiatry*, **42**, 142–146

Beck, A T, Rush, AJ, Shaw, BF, and Emery, G (1979) *Cognitive Therapy of Depression* New York: The Guilford Press

Beck, AT, Steer, RA, and Garbin, MG (1988) Psychometric properties of the Beck Depression Inventory: Twenty-five years of evaluation *Clinical Psychology Review*, **8**, 77–100

Beck, AT, Ward, DH, Mendelson, M, Mock, JE, and Erbaugh, JK (1961) An inventory for measuring depression *Archives of General Psychiatry*, **4**, 561–571

Beckham, EE (1990) Psychotherapy of depression research at the crossroads: Directions for the 1990s *Clinical Psychology Review*, **10**, 207–228

Blackburn, IM, Bishop, S, Glen, AI, Whalley, LJ, and Christie, JE (1981) The efficacy of cognitive therapy in depression: A treatment trial using cognitive therapy and pharmacotherapy, each alone and in combination *British Journal of Psychiatry,* **139**, 181–189

Brewin, CR (1989) Cognitive change processes in depression *Psychological Review,* **96**, 379–394

Brown, RA and Lewinsohn, PA (1984) A psychoeducational approach to the treatment of depression: comparison of group, individual and minimal contact procedures *Journal of Consulting and Clinical Psychology,* **52**, 774–783

Bunch, ME and Winston, MM (1936) The relationship between the character of the transfer and retroactive inhibition *American Journal of Psychology,* **48**, 598

Burns, DD (1980) *Feeling Good: The New Mood Therapy* New York: Signet

Comer, RJ (1992) *Abnormal Psychology* New York: WH Freeman & Company

Dadds, MR, Bovbjerg, DH, Redd, WH, and Cutmore TRH (1997) Imagery in human classical conditioning *Psychological Bulletin,* **121**, 1–15

de Maré, PB (1972) *Perspectives in group psychotherapy: A theoretical background* London: George Allen & Unwin

Dobson, KS (1989) A meta-analysis of the efficacy of cognitive therapy for depression *Journal of Consulting and Clinical Psychology,* **57**, 414–419

Duckham, S, Oei, TPS, and Free, ML (1989) Does Cognitive-Behaviour Therapy support a cognitive model of depression? *Behaviour Change,* **6**, 70–75

Elkin, I, Shea, T, Imber, S, Pilkonis, P, Sotsky, S, Glass, D, Watkins, J, Leber, W, and Collins, J (1989) National Institute of Mental Health treatment of depression collaborative research program: General effectiveness of treatments *Archives of General Psychiatry,* **49**, 971–982

Ellis, A (1962) *Reason and Emotion in Psychotherapy* New York: Lyle Stewart

Ellis, A and Greiger, R (Eds) (1977) *Handbook Of Rational-Emotive Therapy* (Vol 1), New York: Springer

Ellis, A and Harper, RA (1975) *A New Guide to Rational Living* Englewood Cliffs, NJ: Wilshire

Endicott, J and Spitzer, RL (1979) Use of the RDC and SADS in the study of the affective disorders *American Journal of Psychiatry,* *136*, 52–56 And 1978

Fennell, MJ (1989) Depression In K Hawton, PM Salkovskis, J Kirk, & DM Clark (eds) *Cognitive Behaviour Therapy for Psychiatric Problems: A Practical Guide* (pp 169–234) Oxford: Oxford University Press

Fennell, MJV and Teasdale, JD (1987) Cognitive therapy for depression: Individual differences and the process of change *Cognitive Therapy and Research,* **11**, 253–271

First, MB, Spitzer, RL, Gibbon, M, and Williams, JBW (1996) *Structured Clinical Interview for DSM-IV Axis I Disorders, Clinician Version (SCID-CV)* Washington, DC: American Psychiatric Press

First, MB, Spitzer, RL, Gibbon, M, and Williams, JBW (1997) *Structured Clinical Interview for DSM-IV Axis I Disorders, Research Version, Patient/Non-patient Edition (SCID-I/P)* New York: Biometrics Research, New York State Psychiatric Institute

Free, ML and Oei, TP (1989) Biological and psychological processes in the treatment and maintenance of depression *Clinical Psychology Review,* **9**, 653–688

Free, ML, Oei, TPS and Appleton, C (1998) Biological and Psychological processes in recovery from depression during cognitive therapy *Journal of Behavior Therapy & Experimental Psychiatry,* **29**, 213–226

Free, ML, Sanders, MR and Oei, TPS (1991) Treatment outcome of a group cognitive therapy program for depression *International Journal of Group Psychotherapy,* **41**(4), 533–547

Freeman, A (1983) *Cognitive Therapy with Couples and Groups* New York: Plenum

Hawgood, G (1998) Outcome of a One-day workshop cognitive therapy treatment. Unpublished Master of Clinical Psychology Thesis. Brisbane: Griffith University

Hawgood and Free (1999) Outcome of a One-day workshop cognitive therapy treatment: Manuscript in preparation

Hickling, EJ and Blanchard, EM (1997) The private practice psychologist and manual-based treatments: post-traumatic stress disorder secondary to motor vehicle accidents *Behaviour Research & Therapy*, **35**, 191–204

Hollon, SD, DeRubeis, RJ, Evans, MD, Tuason, VB, Wiemer, MJ, Garvey, MJ, and Grove, WM (1988) Cognitive therapy, pharmacotherapy, and combined cognitive-pharmacotherapy in the treatment of depression: I Differential Outcome Unpublished Manuscript, Vanderbilt University

Hollon, SD, Evans, MD, and DeRubeis, RJ (1988) Preventing relapse following treatment for depression: The cognitive pharmacotherapy project In TM Field, PM McCabe, & N Schniederman (Eds) *Stress and Coping Across Development* New York: Erlbaum

Hollon, SD and Kendall, PC (1980) Cognitive self-statements in depression: Development of an automatic thoughts questionnaire *Cognitive Therapy and Research*, **4**, 383–395

Jacobson, NS, Follette, WC, and Revenstorf, D (1984) Psychotherapy outcome research: methods for reporting variability and evaluating clinical significance *Behavior Therapy*, **15**, 336–352

Jacobson, NS and Revenstorf, D (1988) Statistics for assessing the clinical significance of psychotherapy techniques: Issues, problems, and new developments *Behavioral Assessment*, **10**, 133–146

Jarrett, RB and Nelson, RO, (1987) Mechanisms of change in cognitive therapy of depression *Behavior Therapy*, **18**, 227–241

Jones, RG (1969) A factored measure of Ellis' irrational belief system, with personality and maladjustment correlates Doctoral dissertation Texas Technical College (University Microfilms No 69–6443)

King, NJ (1997) Empirically validated treatments and AACBT *Behaviour Change*, **14**, 2–5

Lazarus, AA (1961) Group therapy of phobic disorders by systematic desensitisation *Journal of Abnormal and Social Psychology*, **63**, 505–510

Lewinsohn, PM, Antonuccio, DO, Steinmetz, JL and Teri, L (1984) *The Coping with Depression Course: a Psychoeducational Intervention for Unipolar Depression* Eugene, Oregon: Castilia Publishing Company

Lewinsohn, PM, Muñoz, RF, Youngren, M and Zeiss, AM (1986) *Control Your Depression* New York: Prentice Hall Press

Linehan, MM (1993) *Cognitive-behavioral Treatment of Borderline Personality Disorder* New York: The Guilford Press

McMullin, RE (1986) *Handbook of Cognitive Therapy Techniques* New York: WH Norton and Company

McMullin, RE and Casey, B (1997) *Talk Sense to Yourself* Lakewood, CO: Counseling Research Institute

McMullin, RE and Giles, TR (1981) *Cognitive-behavior Therapy: A Restructuring Approach* New York: Grune and Stratton

Meichenbaum, DH (1974) *Cognitive Behavior Modification* Morristown, NJ: General Learning Press

Miller, RC and Berman, JS (1983) The efficacy of cognitive behavior therapies: A quantitative review of the research evidence *Psychological Bulletin*, **94**, 39–53

Murphy, GE, Simons, AD, Wetzel, RD, and Lustman, PJ (1984) Cognitive therapy and pharmacotherapy: Singly and together in the treatment of depression *Archives of General Psychiatry*, **41**, 33–41

Nietzel, MT, Russell, RL, Hemmings, KA, and Gretter, ML (1987) Clinical significance of psychotherapy for unipolar depression: A meta-analytic approach to social comparison *Journal of Consulting and Clinical Psychology*, **55**, 156–161

Oei, TPS and Free, ML (1995) Does cognitive behaviour therapy validate cognitive models of mood disorders? A review of the empirical evidence *International Journal of Psychology*, **30**, 145–179

Ollendick, TH (1995) AABT and empirically validated treatments *The Behavior Therapist,* **18**, 81–89

Paul, GL, and Shannon DT (1966) Treatment of anxiety through systematic desensitisation in therapy groups *Journal of Abnormal Psychology,* **71**, 124–135

Rachman, S (1966a) Studies in desensitisation II: Flooding *Behaviour Research & Therapy,* **16**, 1–6 (a)

Rachman, S (1966b) Studies in desensitisation III: Speed of generalization *Behaviour Research & Therapy,* **16**, 7–15 (b)

Rimm, DC and Masters JC (1979) *Behavior therapy: Techniques and empirical findings* (2nd edn) New York: Academic Press

Robinson, LA, Berman, JS and Neimeyer, RA (1990) Psychotherapy for the treatment of depression: A review of the controlled outcome research *Psychological Bulletin,* **108**, 30–49

Rush, AJ, Beck, AT, Kovacs, M and Hollon, S (1977) Comparative efficacy of cognitive therapy and pharmacotherapy in the treatment of depressed outpatients *Cognitive Therapy and Research,* **1**, 17–37

Sank, L I and Shaffer, C S (1984) *A Therapist's Manual for Cognitive Behavior Therapy in Groups* New York: Plenum Press

Segal, ZV and Swallow, SR (1994) Cognitive assessment of unipolar depression: Measuring products, processes, and structures *Behaviour Research and Therapy,* **32**, 147–157

Shaffer, CS, Shapiro, J, Sank, LI and Coghlan, DJ (1981) Positive changes in depression, anxiety, and assertion following individual and group cognitive behaviour therapy intervention. *Cognitive Therapy and Research* **5**, 149–157

Shapiro, J, Sank, L, Shaffer, CS and Donovan, DC (1982). Cost effectiveness of individual vs group cognitive behavior therapy for problems of depression in an HMO population. *Journal of Clinical Psychology* **38**, 674–677

Simons, AD, Garfield, SL and Murphy, GE (1984) The process of change in cognitive therapy and pharmacotherapy for depression: Changes in mood and cognition *Archives of General Psychiatry,* **41**, 45–51

Simons, AD, Levine, JL, Lustman, PJ and Murphy, GE (1984) Patient attrition in a comparative outcome study of depression: A follow-up report *Journal of Affective Disorders,* **6**, 163–173

Spitzer, RL and Endicott, J, (1978) *Structured Interview Schedule for Affective Disorders and Schizophrenia* (3rd edn) New York: New York State Psychiatric Institute

Spitzer, RL, Endicott, J and Robins, E (1978) Research diagnostic criteria: Rationale and Reliability *Archives of General Psychiatry,* **35**, 773–782

Spitzer, RL, Endicott, J and Robins, E (1985) *Research Diagnostic Criteria for a Selected Group of Functional Disorders* (3rd edn) New York: New York State Psychiatric Institute

Spitzer, RL and Williams, JBW, (1985) *Structured Clinical Interview for DSM-III-R–Patient Edition (SCID-P, 7/1/85)* New York: New York State Psychiatric Institute

Spitzer, RL, Williams, JBW, Gibbon, M and First, M (1985) *Instruction Manual for the Structured Clinical Interview for DSM-III-R (SCID 7/1/85 Revision)* New York: New York State Psychiatric Institute

Spitzer, RL, Williams, JBW, Gibbon, M and First, M (1990a) *Structured Clinical Interview for DSM-III-R–Patient Edition (SCID-P, Version 10)* Washington DC: American Psychiatric Press

Spitzer, RL, Williams, JBW, Gibbon, M and First, M (1990b) *User's Guide for the Structured Clinical Interview for DSM-III-R* Washington DC: American Psychiatric Press

Teasdale, JD, Fennell, MJ, Hibbert, GA and Amies, PL (1984) Cognitive therapy for major depressive disorder in primary care *British Journal of Psychiatry,* **144**, 400–406

Watson D, and Clark LA (1991) *The Mood and Anxiety Questionnaire* Unpublished Manuscript, University of Iowa, Department of Psychology, Iowa City

Watson, D, Clark, LA, Weber, K, Strauss, ME and McCormick, RA (1995) Testing a tripartite model: II Exploring the symptom structure of anxiety and depression in students, adults and patient samples. *Journal of Abnormal Psycholohy,* **104**, 15–25

Weissman, MM (1978) Development and validation of the Dysfunctional Attitude Scale Paper presented at the Annual Meeting of the Association for the Advancement of Behavior Therapy, Chicago

Williams, JMG (1992) *The Psychological Treatment of Depression: A Guide to the Theory and Practice of Cognitive Behaviour Therapy* (2nd edn) London & New York: Routledge

Wilson, GT, (1997) Treatment manuals in clinical practice *Behaviour Research and Therapy,* **35**, 205–210

Wolpe, J (1997) *The Practice of Behavior Therapy* (4th edn) New York: Pergamon Press

Young, J (1990) *Cognitive Therapy for Personality Disorders: A Schema-focused Approach* Sarasota, Florida: Professional Resource Exchange

INDEX